Shattered By Shackles

Carlton Clay

CEO - Darrell King
COO/Marketing Mngr. Elbert Jones Jr.
KJ Publications, Inc.
www.kjpublications.com
"The Evolution Of Street"

KJ PUBLICATIONS

CEO: DARRELL KING

COO: ELBERT JONES JR.

Currently accepting the following titles…

Urban/Street

Non-fiction

Romance

Erotica

Horror

Mystery

Teen

No children's books at this time

I

From the penology and sociologic perspective – this is a society that offers food, shelter, and clothing for some of the most truculent and volatile people on this planet. These incarcerated men and women have murdered your relatives, raped or molested your women and children, and pillaged, robbed and destroyed your priceless possessions and goods. In addition to that, they have even instilled fear, trepidation, trauma, and an unforgiving wound in your heart.

How can a convicted felon truly understand their victims and their families' pain, grief, hate antipathy, and most importantly their psychological scars that the criminals, perpetrators, and ex-offenders brought upon their life? How can the victims and their families begin the process of forgiving a complete stranger or anyone who've indelibly scarred them emotionally and psychologically; moreover, caused their lives to be shattered and torn to pieces with remnants of debris everywhere. Most criminals will not consider the pain and anguish they've caused on other people's lives because their mindset primarily focuses on the rapaciousness of their plight and motive to fulfill their agenda, schemes, scams, rage, vendettas or gratifying plots. Some criminals have a moral compass in addition to their conscience of course, but the vast majority are unconscionable and unsympathetic – they simply don't care what type of negative or traumatic impact or experience they'll have on people's lives. The apathy of their actions is attributed to the degree of their mentality. However, their recalcitrance should be contained and confined to an environment that is befitted to isolate that sort of evil from permeating in the free society that believes in a civilized civic society in which they can co-exist.

A cage was designed to contain and have constraints over something, and sometimes the only way you can manage and tame an animal is by restricting the free will to do as they please. If this sort of displacement can work for an animal despite the psychological defects, then maybe it's the best ideal location to place an incorrigible human in a cage that can be contained, controlled, or managed while giving them the free will to do as they please.

The "prison society" will either destabilize your mental conditions, exacerbate your problems, plague you with criminalistics stance in pursuant to furthering your criminal endeavors more wisely, or reform and transform you by the drive of your desire and willingness to make conducive sacrifices to change. Once you finally realize the privileges that you've taken for granted, the people you've hurt, the years you've lost, and the remaining time you have left on this planet – the most sensible and reasonable question you would have to ask yourself is, "was all this worth it?" Was being a sync on the streets the true embodiment of your karma for which your transgressions and indiscretions consequently led you to a prison cell, and if so, is your expiation going to be your salvation or will your existence simply be a pig's fart that blows as the dust blows from the ground once you depart from this planet.

In prison, a day can seem like a week if you allow the tedium and monotony to control the stimuli of your brain activities. Each day, there's a considerable amount of idle time and what you do with your time will essentially determine what you'll learn to accept as the reality of your circumstances. The prison society is filled with individuals who store and harbor animosity, hostility, and aggression; therefore harnessing negative energy is the psychodynamics which is seemingly characterized to be ascribed to incorrigible miscreant prisoners. At any given second, an uproar of violence can be displayed, and your peace of mind can be interrupted or distracted by turmoil and strife. When you confine a bunch of predators in a congested location — you can just imagine how tense the environment can be. This is precisely why the prison officials have the emergency task force response teams, in which their operational tactics allow them to effectively respond in a manner to contain disruptive or assaultive incidents.

In prison, predators normally don't attack other predators unless it's either a territorial dispute, an infringement of the prison codes, rivalry disputes or the dominion of the predatory sovereignty of reputational credentials. Predators will always reign over the weakling or prey, and in the prison society, it's the ideal milieu for predators to feed off the prey because obviously the prey are trapped within the confinements of the adversarial predators. Not everyone in the prison society believes in those labels and categories because you have prisoners who are neither prey nor predator and admittedly they are respected and left alone because they are men. In prison, being an adult doesn't make you a man — the qualities of your conduct make you a man and some men are cold-blooded killers, but they're not part of the predatory nonsense that occurs in prison.

When you are engulfed and surrounded by a bunch of degenerate leeches and unscrupulous parasites, it's quite difficult to remain focus on trying to self-rehabilitate because prisons aren't incorporated with a catalyst in a system to offer help to reform you. Prisons are built with political agendas to simply house criminals to gain a profit of appeal to the sentiments of the main emphasis that they propagandize to the public. This notion of proactively trying to keep criminals off the streets slogan is simply political hogwash and a smokescreen because the irony of all this is — crime and criminals are big business for everyone, and quite frankly it keeps a lot of people employed. The primary objective that's being disseminated to the public is, keeping criminals off the streets while containing and confining them, and the secondary political agenda unbeknownst to the public – is to keep the convicted felons in prison as long as they can so the profiteer can enjoy profiting advantages of housing each prisoner. This isn't a political conspiracy theory – the facts are available to anyone who wants to invest their time to research and find out the truth. The politicians and departmental overseers of the state prison systems will only offer what they feel is required or necessary that correlates with their budget. Politicians don't want the exposure of debunking the true facts of exposing the big picture behind the politics of why prisons are being built exponentially and the objectified financial budget to warrant the determination to keep the vast majority of the prisoner's incarcerated. The only necessary provisions they'll offer that's equivalent to necessity is food and clean linen, and they'll buy the cheapest processed meats, vegetables and rotate the bedraggled linen, so they practically won't lose out on a profit. If you're persistent, you might get a piece of paper stating you completed a class for the janitorial classes or received your G.E.D., but that's the extent of any help you'll receive from the prison administration – everything else you must figure out independently to reform, cultivate and make rehabilitative strides for the betterment of yourself.

There is a sad but understandable moral turpitude of a stigma attached to all criminals. As a criminal, everything about you is questionable from a dubious resonating point of view. Your credibility is shattered in shambles, and it's quite convoluted to re-invent yourself with these rigid constraints of the very limited feasible resources. It's as if the system is designed to impede or stifle any pursuits of your endeavors to change. Even when you cordially and humbly inquire about certain discrepancies of the prison official unit-heads – their reactions are retorted with what appears to be a defensive response oppose to a proactive response. The prison administrations don't want you in contact with the outside world within the parameters of matching changes for the betterment of the prisoner's morale and integrity. The general consensus is that it's better and befitting to keep prisoners conformed to the down-trodden compliant mentality oppose to helping prisoners to be more educated. The more educated prisoners become, the more likely they'll be able to identify the impropriety malfeasance and misappropriated funds that are spent for the reasons that are not requested by the state for educational programs, etc. Education is a pivotal aspect of rehabilitating anyone, and if the government de-emphasized on those outlandish policies, they would see a tremendous difference in the positive realms of criminals converting to law-abiding citizens. You certainly can't change or help a breed of people if you don't educate them to learn productive alternative ways to survive. Of course, there have been some fortunate prisoners who've made a difference in their lives and have had a profound effect and impact on others. However, the statistics are staggering, and the perpetuity of this cycle of the generational lineage in this penal system is disparaging and discouraging.

As I sit reposing on the bunk that I've designated to, my thoughts tend to wander into different places, whereas I've learned to cope with the reality of my imagination being a positive reinforcement to stay mentally afloat. What troubles me the most is how so many young black souls such as myself are sitting in a cage for being a youthful fool without proper wings to fly while jumping out of the nest as a naïve baby bird falling to our own demise. Most of us prisoners have been misguided, misinformed and bred with a mentality that's utterly abstract from what is righteous. Undeniably, we are responsible and culpable for our actions, and despite being a product of our environment, it shouldn't be an excuse to undercut the reality of the mental faculty we possess to make the distinction between what's right or wrong. It is imperative that we own up to our foolish indiscretions and mistakes to God because silence or denial can inevitably lead to regression or repetitious behavior of sinful ways. Acknowledging the problem without equally acknowledging the solution is a disservice especially if you're not even willing to do anything about it to change.

I never thought I would appreciate the privilege of silence and serenity until I came to prison. Sometimes, I wait until everyone is asleep in the deep hours of the night so I can enjoy the brief period of silence and placidity. Even in the deep hours of the night, you can hear an echo of snoring coming from different directions like some sort of synchronized symphony. I try to close my eyes and go into a meditative trance to place myself out of this prison world. Everything about this place is a constant reminder of where you're at. If the prisoners are quiet, then the c/o will make enough noise either by jiggling their keys, slamming the doors or tray slots or just speaking on their state-issued walkie-talkies around 3 a.m. in the mornings. Meditation is even dispensed at 3 a.m. as the c/o, and the nurse will be carrying on a conversation as if they don't have any consideration or courteousness that the prisoners are trying to sleep. Trying to have a peaceful state of mind is involute beyond words sometimes, and without some sort of spiritual guidance – Satan will devour you, and then regurgitate you, simply for the satisfaction of watching you flux with aggravation and bitterness.

You would never know how much you would appreciate your freedom until it's taken away from you. No matter how much money you've acquired over the years or how many cars, houses and material things you acquire – in addition to all your criminalistics accomplishments; all the success, money and infamy can be stripped from you in a blink of an eye if you're committing crimes. You would have to ask yourself, "would I rather be rich by the means of illicit, unlawful acts to enjoy a brief period of time in my life just to eventually get caught and go to prison for the rest of my life or a considerable amount of years OR would I rather work hard for a living in a legitimate way but still have my physical freedom." Unfortunately, most criminals especially criminals who are in pursuit of making money – don't get high – they think money is their freedom and without it, it's equivalent to their imprisonment, so their rationalization and rationale is "the risk is simply required for the reward to obtain the money to survive."

If you're an avaricious fool, it's pretty self-explanatory what your answer will be, but if you're wise – your decision should be predicated by making the right decision because ultimately it boils down to a choice. Giving up your volition to choose can be mind-boggling because it takes you back to the basics of your existence as if you're under parental supervision with enforced rules and regulations. Obviously, when you're a child, your choices and options are appropriately administered by your guardian and your "will" to choose is limited; therefore going back to those embryonic stages is as if you're placing an adult under the restrictions of a child to some degree. As we know quite too well – we've all heard the expression that "I'm a grown ass man or woman now," wherefore it is fair to assume that adults generally don't like to be told what to do. No matter how temperamental or aggressive you may be, in the prison society, you will be told what to do, and like a child, you will face the disciplinary consequences for not doing what you were instructed to do. When you see all the simple privileges that you once had as a physically free adult taken away from you, absorbing that reality in itself can take you through a world- wind of conflicting emotions.

Prison is a society where despair, violence, aggression, loneliness, depression and spiritual paralysis are all intertwined in one. For some prisoners, doing time is a natural affinity for them because they've spent practically their entire life in juvenile detentions, institutions and they graduated to the adult prison system. An adult prison is a by-product of an upgrade for those sort of prisoners and the juvenile facilities only prepared them for the adult prison system. Certain prisoners may not be able to function productively or cope beyond the realms of the gates that they've been confined to for a significant portion of their life. It's senseless to even try to have a dialogue or any discussion with the individuals who are either delusional or feed themselves an illusion for the sake of an argument because it is degrading in prison to imply or insinuate that a person may be institutionalized remotely; however the immutable fact is, some prisoners in their own befuddlement will not broach this topic due to the daunting reality of their circumstances.

The new intakes AKA "The New Fish of the Sea" are curious and uncertain as to what world they've just entered. They really don't know what to expect, and they only know what they've heard and seen on prison movies, or they base some of their local jail experiences as a leg to walk on in prison. Initially, the new intakes can be influenced and manipulated by the veteran prisoners because they're gullible and susceptible. The scavengers of the prison literally wait upon the new arrivals because the scavengers survive by means of the manipulative tactics and strategies in which intimidation and other factors could be the methodology of their exploitative pursuit for the new arrival. Of course, not all veteran prisoners are poisonous dissolute vultures but the majority of them are, and this is the reason that makes the prison society a snakes' pit. The majority of any type of belief or indoctrination can dominate a system, a culture, a society and a nation. A new arrival is like a new opportunity to gain something that you don't have because most of the time new intakes still have active resources and loved ones that haven't disavowed or detached themselves from the commencement of their journey of incarceration. Very early in the prison bid, family and friends are likely to be supportive until the reality hit their psyche that this is no longer a symbiosis, in which gradually people who once supported you will become an apparition.

Trust is too much of a powerful word to use in prison. It's quite difficult for me to trust anyone and prison has made me realize how much of a privilege it is to have someone in this world that you can confidently trust. Having someone you can trust in this particular system is rare, and quite frankly, it's ill-advised even to consider the notion of trusting someone in prison. There's no need for "trust" in an environment where there's so much deception, chicanery, and manipulation. Sadly to say, most youngsters are lost in their own ambivalence in here, and they don't know what to do with themselves, so they cling to whatever bolster or catapult to get out of their dejection. Not knowing what course to take could evoke a yearning for someone to trust, for guidance, and understanding, but unfortunately, prison is not an environment that embraces you with love, compassion, and kindness. Young prisoners need guidance and encouragement a bit, so does their victims or youngsters who are not incarcerated but are leading towards a destructive path of a statistic, either by death or imprisonment.

Most prisoner's hide their pain behind this projected image of this nonchalant behavior they exhibit. It's as if by showing any indication of emotional weakness in here — emotional displays will preclude you from being characterized as being strong. Emotional prosperities and tendencies will place you under the gun for scrutiny with a high beam radar as if you're under some sort of profile analysis amongst the others.

I've literally observed a younger person who portrays the image of a defiant renegade, withheld his tears till he was able to get some privacy in his cell to vent and release a cascade of tears. It's difficult for young prisoners to feel like they have to be walking on eggshells every time they take a step because it's psychologically tiresome and exhaustive to be on guard all the time. Inferiority plays a tremendous role in trampling your self-esteem and confidence as a young adult in prison while learning the ropes in uncharted territory.

No one wants to be perceived as a weakling in prison, so most of the time prisoners use coping defense mechanisms, coupled with a façade to protect their image as a way of camouflaging their true feelings with a dissimulated persona. Being disingenuous to survive and cope is unorthodox to me, but not everyone was bred to be firm and tough — some are fickle and weak, hiding behind a pistol. In prison, you don't have the privilege of being an open, gregarious expressive liberal person. One would have to come to terms that there's a certain overtone of a language that's spoken with an unguarded demeanor with the sentiments of being resolute and firm. There's nothing wrong with camaraderie, but that should be an authentic, spontaneous diachrony, in which time will enable both parties to evaluate the authenticity of one's personality traits. You don't have to drop your guards to have a comrade or an associate in prison, but at the same time, it's ill-advised to allow your emotions to determine your decisions to prematurely embrace anyone in prison, or in life.

I've asked myself, "what is a bond?" and "what are the criterion to establish a bond?" Just like in the free world, there must be a common denominator of interest and a commonality between prisoners. In prison, establishing a bond is a typical occurrence because it gives the prisoner the opportunity to clique with one another in the social dichotomy within these prison gates. You must be discreet about who you allow yourself to establish a bond with because an instigator or a knucklehead can stir up some nonsense which can automatically be an invitation for you to be a part of a potential quarrelsome conflict or physical altercation. When other prisoners recognize your associate as your comrade — whenever a potential conflict is about to occur — you may be a target for the associate attack as well. You may not be a direct target, but you are a target·by association and affiliation nonetheless.

Each day, everyone is observing the individuals in their surroundings, and everyone tries to identify with whom they could be a potential threat and who's non-threatening. A person who's characterized as a non-threatening individual, usually, that particular individual exemplify some form of weakness. However, sometimes the prisoners AKA (convicts) may perceive an individual as a non-threatening person and when the convict attempt to test the validity of their observation by some form of disrespect or encroachment, subsequently, that particular non-threatening person may display an aggressive, combative side of the caliber that the convict didn't expect them to have. Misunderstanding or misperceiving a person in prison can get another prisoner seriously hurt or even murdered. The youngsters in prison are careless and reckless, and they're prone to cause some sort of provocation because they're more inclined to channel their supposed aggression destructively and counter-productively.

If you take a young recalcitrant individual and you restrict their ability to be able to do as they please, naturally they're going to rebel. Young temperamental individuals struggle with their contumacy with authority figures, and their behavioral problems will continue to escalate until they're able to come to the realization that their oppositional ways will not be tolerated at all. In prison, you would have no choice but to learn to be compliant and patient if you don't want to spend a considerable amount of time in administrative segregation AKA "The Hole." The hole is specifically for disciplinary reasons, but there's a number of reasons you can be placed in the hole. In the beginning, you may have those individuals who will try to break the rules and regulations flagrantly but in due time, they'll either start to comply with the rules and regulations or get smarter in manipulating the rules or regulations, or they'll continue to have episodic incidents of violating the rules throughout the entire duration of their incarceration. Either way, only a fool will continue to be foolish.

At one time, criminals went to prison and cultivated themselves. They read more, they study more, and if they weren't working on their mind, they were working on their body and spirit. Of course you've always had the maladjusted misfits and knuckleheads, but for the most part, prisoners abide by the prison codes of conduct amongst other convicts. In this day and age, the majority of the prisoners don't even think about picking up a book. They would rather watch T.V., play tabletop and board games all day long or masturbate every opportunity they can or a combination of all three. Not to sound like I am glorifying or sensationalize these internal prison codes of respect, loyalty, and honor. In other words, I'm currently a part of the statistics, but I simply refuse to be a conformist or to allow my brain cells to go to waste with the futility of idle stimulation. I've been ingrained with certain qualities as a child and for the most part, what I was taught coincided with loyalty, integrity, and principles of the street codes but of course the instilment of negative aspects were a defilement that imbued my discretion and compromises my judgment.

Prison codes and even street codes may be opaque and abstract to the normative of the people in the free world society but (prison is a society in itself) of course a lot of the prison codes and the street codes have been ignored by the newer generation of prisoners. In addition to that, the A.C.L.U, the U.S. Dept. of Justice and the A.C.A. have facilitated and advocated for new implementations to ensure the safety of prisoners, confidential informants and so forth. The prison official and administrator vehemently express their low tolerance for cruel punishment on prisoners received by other prisoners when they broke the prison codes. Vile deviants have been raping, extorting and exploiting prisoners for decades and the court system was overwhelmed by lawsuits from prisoner's family members — that's why the courts have incorporated strict civil suit procedures to essentially minimize the paper trail from entering the state and federal court system. Unfortunately, death can be the penalty if a certain prison code is broken, but in the Virginia prison system, this sort of fatality doesn't occur that often. You may see an inmate in the same pod with his co-defendant that testified against him, and his co-defendant is untouched with impunity. However, in other prison systems, his co-defendant would have been attacked on sight of his arrival or a few hours later. When I first came to the Virginia prison system — snitches and child molesters were dealt with violently, in terms of physical and psychological affliction, persecution and so forth. Of course, the prison system stats are different, in terms of location and security levels with the violence decreasing or increasing, but whatever what the statistics may be, it doesn't change the caliber of the individuals you're surrounded by and the unpredictability of what may occur at any given second. The tedium of the prison cycle throughout the day to day activities can make some prisoners desperate for any sort of fulfillment or gratification — depending on the prisoner. Most prisoners are incarcerated for some sort of drug-related crime, whether they used the drugs, sold the drugs or the drug led them to commit robbery, murder or even rape. The undeniable factor is — most of the crimes are committed as a result of drugs playing a role in their criminal actions.

Prisoners become extremely desperate for drugs in prison because the monotony of the confinement triggers their addictive traits heavily, especially if the prisoner is aware that drugs are available on the compound of the prison. Sometimes, a prisoner will use desperate measures to get their hands on drugs and consequently that could ignite a lot of conflicts and confrontational nonsense. At some prisons, the accessibility of having drugs is a privilege to those who have the most money and resources in prison but there's always a scoundrel indigent predator waiting to seize on an opportunity of a prey, or whomever they think can potentially open window to obtain drugs. The escapism of the mind can be perilous with the practice of using drugs to cope, to function, or to maintain a distorted stability — it's all psychological. Drugs are the devil's entrapment and tools to have dominion over your life and unfortunately a lot of people detrimentally lose out on their years on this planet before they can kick these destructive addictions.

In prison, it's difficult not to be distracted because there's so much negativity as it's floating in the air. Negative energy can have a contagious effect on people, whereas they're prone to absorb, abreact, and respond in accordance with the atmosphere and milieu they're in. You can be antisocial and socially withdrawn to the degree of isolating yourself completely from the negative nonsensical foolishness that occurs in the prison society, but unless you're in segregation, AKA "The Hole," your reclusivity will be interfered with. Whether pondering over the homosexual indulgements and disputes, or having disruptive behavioral problems or indulging in gang activities, or perpetuating the chase of the chemical induced high — all of these practices are mundanely counterproductive especially while being incarcerated. Either way, it's not conducive, and it's certainly a destructive regressive cycle that will lead to the perpetuity of your imprisonment or demise.

I think in the beginning, most of the prisoners who were raised up in the ghetto will have a difficult time trying to adjust to following the rules and regulations; however being able to adapt and acclimate oneself to an uncharted environment is somewhat different. Being a product of your underprivileged neighborhoods can pose some difficulties psychologically in terms of complying with the constraints of the prison rules and regulations; wherefore the disciplinary segregation is a most unavoidable in the regards to being placed in the hole for some sort of disciplinary offense. When the reality hits you — this is when you will inevitably determine if you want to continue to do things your way or become wiser for the betterment of yourself in accordance to what's right. Either way, there are choices to be made.

Sometimes, we're placed in an unavoidable situation while being in prison and it's disfavorable to be perceived as a coward because the continuity of the affront or disrespect will be punctuated by the incident that we didn't defend the dignity of our respect for. Of course our pride plays a role in the equation, but at the same time, disrespect can affect your image; moreover, your self-dignity as a man in prison. You are required to be firm and stand uprightly in a predatory environment because there's no room for gray areas for timidity or cowardice. It's a lot easier for some people to say, "Don't feed into their ignorance," or "Don't allow your pride to get in the way from being humbled to walk away from a potential conflict." Humility and civility can be the detriment of your decision-making process in certain instances, whereas the virtue of meekness is to a docile reaction and response. Humility is an excellent virtue to apply in our lives, but not in prison — humility could be a disadvantage or Achilles heel if you're too humble because prisoners will try to take advantage of your humbleness. These deviants and parasites will suck your blood dry to the bone like a nefarious scavenger, only if you allow them to and that's the garden variety in prison and in the free world.

Most prisoners depend and rely on their families and friends to be their emotional and financial crutch and contrary to what people may think — 3 hots and a cot is resoundingly inadequate to sustain one's sanity. The outside support can essentially keep your mind intact, whereas this form of stability could preclude you from going haywire. There's a manifold of ways to block your reality out, but inevitably, the gravitational pull of the earth will force you to face your reality. The prison society doesn't offer a lot of options; therefore your survival is on the basis of maintaining some type of mental or spiritual balance. Your stability is pivotal in prison because the banality of the repetition on the day to day activities can be deleterious for your mind in which it's quite common for prisoners to distort and delude their own minds to cope with their own reality. Undeniably, any form of imprisonment is a psychological and spiritual war punctuated by your desire or drive to live and to survive. You can either choose to productively do the time by the way of educating yourself, for the betterment of utilizing the time that you have to reform yourself intellectually or spiritually, or you can let the time do you, by playing games or getting involved in counterproductive activities – either way, you have the volition. Problems and conflicts will definitely occur and even when you're trying to be productive – there's always the possibility of an agitator causing a distraction, whereas they try to interfere with the very sanctuary of stability that you've created.

Prison is a dysfunctional environment for anyone to try and cultivate themselves because the demonizing energy that's being plagued and harnessed in here is like a contagious virus. In order to remain focus on your positive objective and goals while serving time, it's imperative that you focus and disaffiliate yourself with anyone who's not in sync with your progression of making strides to ameliorate and change. Camaraderie can be empowerment if your comrade is driven by faith to change his ways – otherwise, having a comrade in prison can be a liability because your association in here can play a major role in the sense of the domino effect of what your comrade chooses to get involved which with may directly affect you negatively.

A lot of people couldn't even imagine themselves being locked up and the truth of the matter is that freedom is a privilege that can't be taken for granted. In this country, freedom is a choice, and if you choose to be free, then your choices and decisions should coincide with not committing crimes, waking up every day and being committed to working legitimately, and this requires discipline, especially when you have to tolerate with colleagues and constituents that vexes you and interfere with the daily function of your job descriptions. Unfortunately, in most cases, you are required to tolerate the conditions whatever it may be if you want to remain employed, because if you're not employed legitimately, then you're doing something illicitly. Unlawful acts suggest you don't respect your freedom enough to abide by the laws of the land. Of course, you don't have to be vexed in an intense working environment to define your discipline to work for a living. Personally, I have a significant amount of admiration for those who were once exposed and engaged in the illegal activities but then choose to give up the lifestyle of the quick dollar just for the sake of the ones they love wholeheartedly and for appreciating their physical freedom. I also admire those who've worked all of their lives legitimately without compromising their integrity to commit crimes or to curtail or bypass the laws.

Criminal acts can become addictive, and the love for money can ruin your entire life. Most people would prefer to make quick money with practically no physical demands, oppose to working a grueling job or just simply a nine to five with the consistent time frame requiring you to be there. The cupidity of a fool would risk or jeopardize their freedom to make quick cash, but when they get caught, they try to sell their souls to avoid prison time. Crime coincides with greed intertwined with the desires of the flesh and the pleasures of what's gained by who is the committing the crime. There are millions of criminals in the world who will probably never step their foot in a prison cell because they break the laws in a way that it's either too petty to be recognized, or they have too much money to be caught, or it's commonly done as a way of living in which prosecution isn't pursued. Either way, laws are made to be broken and the irony of this concept – some people actually want people to break the laws so they can prosper and reap the benefits from your criminal acts in some type of capacity.

Prison is a world where your existence only exists by those who truly love you. Your despair, your despondency, and your emptiness is a testament of one side of the spectrum in your life. No matter how much you've matured or changed, people will always look down on you because you're indelibly marked as an ostracized wretched infested animal. Considering the tremendous negative impact criminals have had on people over the centuries, it's understandable why people, in general, detest criminals. If you're labeled or characterized as a criminal – you are a pariah whether you know it or not and depending on the crime that you have committed, a lot of people, in general, don't even want to have any dealings with you. A criminal act can besmirch your reputation and stigmatize you for the rest of your life, and quite frankly, there's no need to try to destigmatize people's perspective when God loves you despite any of your past iniquities.

In prison, each day is a constant reminder of where you may spend the rest of your life or at least a good portion of your life, and the reality of your inept circumstances can make your bones throb. A lot of prisoners don't even care about what's going to happen in the next five years, and they're not also trying to prepare themselves to deal with the fact of the prospect of re-entering back into the society one day with a felony on their record. The only thing that matters to most prisoners is making sure they have the means to eat junk food, smoke cigarette, buy music, get high or trying to find ways to lust over females through magazines or any other methods to lust over women or even men. It's almost as if you live in a world/society where people don't want to do anything with their lives besides living in their figment of the imagination of being an aspiring rapper, womanizer or a drug kingpin. You're surrounded by addictive zombies and a bunch of deceptive, manipulative vultures, so there's not a lot of room to breathe in quality air. Prison is like the Dead Sea that's inviably not sustainable, but there's hope with a heartbeat. I committed a crime, so I signed up for this prison society and I've been co-existing with this defilement practically all my life, but there comes a time when you have to change even if you weren't conform to this way of life.

If you wholeheartedly desire to change and revolutionize your way of thinking and living your life, prison makes it more difficult than ever. The only way you can wash away the evil impurities off your flesh cathartically – you would truly need a spiritual awakening to convert your life and have an emotional maturation and spiritual transformation in God's bosom. In prison, we're living in the snake's pit, and when you eventually escape from the pit, then you'll enter the devil's nest, and nothing is possible without God's love. The only way to avoid the negative energy that floats in the air of this hostile environment of prison – you would have to put the armor of God on to shield yourself, and even then you'll still be under attack, whether it's spiritually, financially, emotionally or physically. Trying to remain focus in prison is a very arduous task because you would literally have to be antisocial and the tedium alone can take a toll or you especially if you're young and loquaciously inclined to be amongst your associate.

Without God, it's going to be quite convoluted to work on your short-comings especially in a society that embraces negativity as a way to survive.

Prisons were specifically designed to challenge you in every way possible. Sometimes, a physical altercation can be practically unavoidable, but at the same token, the fray could be necessary to prevent other incidents. Prison will detrimentally challenge you emotionally by keeping you emotionally detached from those you love, and this displacement in itself can asphyxiate your heart especially if you have children. It's heart-rending to watch your child grow up while you're behind a prison gate and I'm sure it's an equal amount of emotional heartaches to watch your child growing up in various institutions and prisons while you're in the free world. Losing a child as a victim of violence may not be tantamount to losing a child to prison, but forgiveness is our salvation either way.

The separation of your loved ones can take you through a world-wind of conflicting emotions, and the psychological toll could be asymptomatic to a downward spiral of stress and depression. There's a psychosomatic process that's incurred when you don't learn effective ways to channel out the unwanted stress and stain on the brain in prison. You can become dispirited, and you will start to give up on the little faith you have in God. Most youngsters perceive faith in God as a form of weakness when you get on your knees to pray. The common perception is "If you didn't pray on the streets, then why start to pray for mercy and deliverance once you get caught and go to prison."

Religious beliefs are controversial topics obviously because just like in the free world, prisoners will adamantly try to confute that their belief system is the only true belief to have. In prison, Christians are commonly perceived as the timid, hypocritical, or the sexually dissolute group of individuals behind these gates. Convicts tend to implant this preconceive notion into the youngster's minds that if you want true salvation, you can only receive it through the faith of Islam rather by Sunni or N.O.I. Muslims. A lot of the younger generations try to degrade the iconic Martin Luther King Jr. because they try to characterize his actions as a person who was too passive and weak to allow anyone to strike at him and he doesn't strike back. I try to disregard their naivetés and ignorance, but truth be told, it's quite offensive when they pontificate this irreverent point of views with this blasphemous disgraceful ingratitude towards the beloved activist that died for the cause. Younger guys want to be socially accepted, so they conform to the normative just for the sake of the status quo. They're more inclined to join a gang or hang around their peers that make them seem cool because subliminal peer pressure plays on the psyche of a pliable young mind.

Religion is no longer taken seriously as it once did, in the sense of the caliber of individuals who are legitimately trying to change and develop a closer relationship with God. Majority of the people in prison use their religious beliefs as an escape hoping if they pray enough times or attend enough religious services, God will shorten the length of their sentence or offer some type of relief for their desperate outcries. It's pathetic for anyone even to attempt to try to beguile God with the senseless chicanery; however in some individual's minds, as long as their actions appear to be genuine then there's a chance of being liberated by God. This is not a new course of action because hypocrites have been around since man came into existence. Prisoners are likely to perceive Christians as a hypocrite than any other religious groups incarcerated because a lot of Christians in the prison system are reprobates. It's commonly perceived that Christians who are incarcerated join the Christians as an outlet to be left alone by the predators because for some odd reason predators don't really target Christians in prison like they target anyone else. There are devout authentic Christians in prison who are not perceived as cowards, and they are serious about their faith in God.

Gangs are running the youth lives because so much defilement is being infused into their young minds that they personify an evil force of energy whereas they gravitate to the despicable individuals who are responsible for wreaking havoc in every corner they can reach.

Just like in the free world, youngsters join gangs for various reasons. In prison — fear, peer pressure, and wanting to be socially accepted while being a part of something, is some of the main reasons why a lot of youngsters join a gang. The flip side of it all, people want to join a gang, but they can't deal with the consequences of their actions when they may have to carry out an act to show and prove their loyalty. Most gang leaders can discern and detect a phony wannabe puppet or guinea pig. A lot of youngsters believe being a part of a gang is like being a part of a family and some of them will subject themselves to demoralizing acts. Gang leaders normally are always trying to recruit new members especially if your membership can be beneficial in which the leaders can sway you or manipulate you out of your money, resources or to have you carry out an act to signify and further illustrate their course of retribution when someone violates. Gang activities are massively spread throughout the United States and abroad, and this trendy epidemic of acceptance is destroying the very fabric of the infrastructure in which our proactive trailblazers have bled and died to make sacrifices for. The youth are disciplined to pick up a book to help educate themselves, but they are more inclined to join a gang.

A lot of citizens in the free world prefer not to know what it's like living behind these prison bars. There's always an explanation as to why people are the way they are and why they exhibit certain personality traits but some people don't want any explanation, and they care less of trying to help any person who've victimized someone. They've earned their right to be free by abiding by the laws of the land and prison is just a place that confines inhumane individuals that chose not to abide by the laws, in which this is how some people feel. People are more concerned with the punishment being imposed and carried out and making sure whatever crime a person has committed — a repeated offense will not occur again. Some people believe gang members are responsible for most of the violent crimes that are committed in the inner cities, and prison is the ideal solution to essentially decrease the violence. Some people even prefer death for the perpetrator as being a solution to get rid of a lot of the gangs in America. Either way, prison is a place where a lot of people in the society think criminals who committed a crime that in some way traumatized a person are kept; those particular criminals should remain in prison until they die. Some people disagree with that mindset, but the fact remains, people are taking a risk when they allow a criminal who has committed a serious crime to come back into the society; therefore considering the trauma we as criminals have caused upon people, I've learned to understand and accept citizens grievous views on criminals in general, regardless if it's stigmatic or stereotypical.

For me, prison is an everyday reflection of why I'm in here. The realization of spending a significant portion of my life in prison is so mind-blogging that just the thought of that alone has paralyzed my spirits at times. I thought I was tough, I thought I could fight any battle, and I thought I had mental fortitude and longanimity, considering all of the ordeals I've endured. I always took on any challenge, and I did not back down from no one, but hurting an innocent person was never a part of the game I signed up for in the streets. Nothing had quite prepared me for dealing with the heart-rending emotional stress of the separation of being incarcerated away from my family. Despite that I had broken laws, I always had moral fiber and a conscience, and I didn't believe in unjustifiably inflicting harm on anyone. My environment and my dysfunctional household played a major role in who I became, but that has no bearings on the fact why I committed a crime. There's no justifiable excuse as to why I broke the law, and despite that, I had absolutely no intentions of hurting anyone — it happens, and I have to live with that for the rest of my life.

Imagine eating next to a person who has decapitated his wife and his children or being in a cell with a person who has raped and murdered teenage girls. There are cold-blooded murderers in here who look ingenuous like an innocent baby face child, and that alone could be scary to people in the society because the television has a bad habit of giving you this depiction of a descriptive profile analysis of what most murderers look like. Police are infamous for their inaccurate profiling based on their racially profiling assessment what they may perceive as suspicious or conspicuously odd. The irony of the status quo – it's contrary to the reality of a murderer profiler because the murderers are much younger now and they appear to be harmless with their adorable innocent looks but in all actuality, they are gruesome and heinous murderers. There is no certain type of look, demeanor, or disposition that a murderer is supposed to have because a lot of people live a double life with multi-personality traits. An honor role gregarious likable extrovert kid can become a cold-blooded, calculating murderer. This same likable kid could have been having homicidal ideations the entire time you've known him or her, but you would never know this because their evil rage could be disguised and dissimulated with a cordial smile. It's sickening and appalling how people hurt innocent people, and there's no excuse or explanations you can give to a grieving family member.

It's hard to trust a murderer, a rapist, or a thief and that certainly doesn't leave too much room for trust in prison considering you're surrounded by those sort of individuals. Murderers, rapists, and thieves should be punished, but what is the appropriate punishment? If you can't trust a criminal, you certainly can't trust a murderer not to murder anyone, you can't trust a thief not to steal anymore, and you certainly can't trust a rapist not to rape anymore. What's the solution if trust is a determining factor with any criminal? Most people think a long duration of imprisonment or even death is a viable, effective solution. There's never an elixir or panacea that will solve all problems and issues because there are reprobates and deplorable that will plague this planet until the end of the human race. There are practical solutions that can essentially minimize the recidivism rate, but the question is — do anyone really wants to invest the time, money and resources to reform a criminal.

Most criminals will not work at a job paying ten dollars an hour on the streets, but in prison, they'll practically beg for a prison job only paying twenty-three cents an hour for the maximum of 30 hours a week. Prisoners will watch you die if they can replace the position you have with a prison job. Some prisoners wouldn't mind if you died just for the sake of seeing who will move in your bed space as a potential prospect for finagling. This sort of apathy of indifference is encompassed with the affinity of loathe and despicable hate which is parallel to the prison society. That may sound like hyperbole or farfetched, but it's quite realistic. Undoubtedly, there are some deranged lunatics in prison, and their mental instability doesn't desist once they enter the prison gates. A demented criminal mental illness may exacerbate once they come to prison and for some prisoners, it would be imprudent and ill-advised to ever release them back into the society. It's ridiculous how pitiful people will become behind these prison walls but the reality of it all, as long as evil exists through the human consciousness, people will suffer, and people will do all sorts of maniacal things whether they're in prison or not. Metaphorically, prison can be prophylaxis, a purgatory or a reformatory to your salvation and deliverance.

When you live in an infested pit along with all sorts of reptiles, while trying to coexist with the moral turpitude of the degeneration of snakes, you will feel this poisonous inflammation affect as you inhale the oxygen breathe. Every day is a constant reminder of how much you hate the environment of prison and the strong abhorrence you carry on your shoulders against the infested rodents that besieges the prison with the bombardment of evil. Hate is a strong word but when you're amongst criminals who enjoy the bereavement of victim's family members — hate is seemingly appropriate especially when you have a conscience being around the vileness. When you're surrounded by people who lie, deceive and manipulate every chance they get, you'll start to feel out of place like a pariah whereas categorically you'll feel utterly disenchanted. You will wrestle and battle with so much regret because it becomes surreal that your criminal lifestyle led you to prison with a bunch of demoralizing vultures and snakes.

Each day, the prison guards count five times a day, and when they commence their count, you're supposed to stand for counts so the guards can easily identify how many people are alive and accounted for in the cells. Most prisoners get used to the whistle when the guard blows it to bring it to your attention that it's count time, but that whistle has become a vexation to my spirits. Each building has a main intercom that's normally used to make important announcements, and the main P.A. system is like a voice out of the sky alerting you to the reality of your imprisonment. If you sleep lightly, you'll inevitably suffer from sleep deprivation over the years because when you're confined in an adjacent location with nearly a hundred prisoners, the crescendo of the level noise can be overwhelming. It's very rare to have a quiet, peaceful day without a bunch of unnecessary ruckus. Being boisterous and noisy is of the norm in prison, and it's almost a privilege to be able to enjoy the quietness while the prisoners are asleep. Every hour of the day, there's an amplified amount of noise, and the noise travels through the walls, the steel doors, and everywhere else. Everything about prison is a constant reflection of what you took for granted, and whether you like it or not for most prisoners, this is their life, and they will inevitably die in here for the victimization of their actions. Is a gruesome criminal worthy of sympathy — probably not because sympathy should be reserved for the innocent. Despite the environment is noisy, the people are antagonizing, and you feel like an immigrant at times – the choices we've made led us here and some of us shouldn't have received lengthy sentences, crime in itself has torn families apart.

The prison life is dull, dreadful, and repetitive, and the stimulation I receive from reading books is mediocre at times. Each prisoner chooses what they do with their time to pre-occupy themselves, but the fact remains, we will all be lost if we don't get in tune with our spirituality. Maturation is a developmental process that takes time and as pathetic as it sounds, some people don't want to grow up – they fear maturity and growth because they're either content or complacent with their silly infantile ways or they just fear change. Whatever the reason is, prison is an environment/society that can drain your fiber out your core wherefore you don't even feel like you're alive. It's a common thing here to repress or suppress your despair, dejection, and pain but you can't hide it from yourself. We've lost our privileges to be physically free, and whether we'll get the opportunity to restore that privilege again, that will be determined in the eventuality of faith, fate, time and God.

Prisoners who take non-threatening individuals and characterize them as a threat, normally that particular person they classify as a threat will carry around a shank because their paranoia could make them become wary or delusional. The most aggressive prisoners will keep a shank on them or nearby, but even the less aggressive timid prisoners keep a shank as well. Fear plays a tremendous role in the willingness to protect yourself and prison can conform you to a savage. Prisoners who have a reputation for stabbing or killing a prisoner, the convicts tend to stay out of their way as respect. The caliber of prisoners in the Virginia prison system isn't as tough or violent than prisoners in other prisons in the U.S., like San Quentin, Lorton for D.C., Marion, or Angola but nonetheless, it's still dangerous. Murder, rape, and robberies do occur in this prison system, but it's not commonly done as much because the main headquarters of Virginia Dept. of Correction has implemented very strict disciplinary sanctions to show they have a very low tolerance for offenses of murder, rape, and robbery.

A veteran convict is usually responsible for the rapes that do occurs in prison, and the convicts mostly target young Caucasian man or timid young men who have some form of a resemblance of a woman in the sense of their features; however sometimes it appears that these deviants don't give a damn what the person looks like if the man doesn't objectively pose any resistance. Usually, roughly 99 percent of the rapes that do occur aren't reported because of the defamatory shame of the rumors that will be spread once the C/Os has awareness of what occurred. If a person is raped, normally the raped offender will ask to go the hole; when the C/O or building supervisor inquire as to why the offender would like to go to the hole – normally the inmate will tell them he's having some family issues or he fears for his life. This method is commonly done in prison to avoid mentioning the truth and also to avoid being labeled as a snitch. The reason why the inmate wouldn't mention their cellmate's name is that it would be pretty obvious once the active supervisor or investigator come to lock his cell-mate up and then he will be labeled as a snitch. Being labeled as a snitch will ostracize and ex-communicate you from practically everyone but then again times are changing since I got locked up. Your status as a snitch can dwindle away depending how much of a resourceful commodity you are.

Administrative segregation is a housing unit that keeps you in a single cell for 24hrs a day most of the time unless it's your day to go outside in the recreation cages or take a shower three times a week. You can be placed in segregation for protective custody, investigative status, mental health status, suicidal watch status or for disciplinary status. Normally, a disciplinary infraction is imposing warrants disciplinary segregation when the offense is classified as a serious offense or major offense. You have minor offenses and major offenses broken down in 100 series which is the major offenses and 200 series which is the minor offenses. The 100 series charges are major offenses like aggravated assault, weapons charges and inciting riots, etc. Sometimes the prison administration will manipulate and circumvent the policies and procedure to ensure that certain influential prisoners are kept in the hole because they feel like this particular prisoner poses some sort of threat to the security of operations. If need be, the prison officials will falsify documents or declare false allegations to justifiably explain their rationale of the determination to transfer certain prisoners to a higher security prison to maintain compliance and order.

Regardless of what mental problems you may have, prisons are equipped to handle the most acute mental illnesses. If one prison is unable to contain you, then you will be transferred congruously to a prison where the C/Os are more qualified and trained to handle a prisoner who's mentally ill or disturbed. Prison is just another form of a psychiatric institution because most prisoners are mentally disturbed, psychologically challenged or struggling with chemical imbalances. Prison is the ideal environment that's befitted to house dangerous criminals and mental patients because of the secure structure of the confinement. It's strikingly unique how steel, metal, and concrete plays on the psyche of the mind especially when you conjoin them together to make a cage of confinement. Initially, every species abreact with the resistance of discomfort but "time" can be your worst enemy or your best friend — in the sense of a curse or a blessing depending on your mindset.

Most of us that are in prison with lengthy sentences are already dead in spirit, and we just wake up each day hoping something will change. With myself, I've matured and changed through my experiences of doing time coupled with God's phenomenal power to help transform me, in which I came to terms with my reality but not conforming to it. There's no way in the world I would ever take anyone through emotional agony of psychological detachment again, and more importantly, I would never be disobedient to God again especially if I'm ever privileged to be free. I was once aggressively violent to any opposition, and I refuse to yield or succumb to any oppressor or demagogue. Prison has made me realized that I was just a lost befuddled young man who had no sense of direction. It's a sad daunting reality how so many fathers and mothers lose their babies to the prison system, but it's even worst to lose your baby by death; either way, the loses are hurtful to the heart. Life can be equivalent to rolling a dice, by allowing fortuity to be your fate, but God gives us the volition to determine if our autonomy will lead us to him to love him.

Prison brings forth spiritual and emotional pain, and life in prison is just a physical hell where you rest your head on a brimstone rock. With the grace and mercy from God, you can be delivered from the devil's oppression, but it's quite difficult and challenging to maintain a grounded balance when you're surrounded by the negativity that you once embraced as a way of life and how you're appalled by it. There have been times when I've questioned myself whether I have a purpose or not and invariably I could avoid this indescribable force deep down in my heart. My heart was torn to pieces from so much evil and negativity, and I wanted to wash this garbage out of my heart cathartically, but I didn't know how or where to begin. I yearned in my heart to show the naysayers that there are some criminals of my caliber who could be reformed and I could offer a significant contribution to the youths that are leading down this path of imprisonment or death. There have been many lonely days and nights when I've dissected my brain from every possible angle, and I definitely concluded that I hated what I've become.

I hated the evil that was ingrained in me; I hated the negative energy that I exuded when I got aggravated or agitated, and I start to hate my outlook and perspective on life. Hate is a strong word, but that's what I felt, and I was so disillusioned with who I've become that the only option was to try to change and revolutionize the way I felt about life, the way I thought and the way I perceived life to be. I harnessed, hoarded and harbored enough negative energy in my core that it murdered me and I wanted to live.

The prison life is like every other daily routine, but the only difference is, it seems like a constant circuitous motion of stagnation. Any given day you wake up, and a new rile is being implemented and enforced, or the entire facility could be placed on a complete lockdown, or you could get stabbed in an unprovoked incident and that could be your last day alive. A lot of prisoners adjust to their environment, and they develop this mental adaptation for their circumstances to cope with their reality; whether they choose to block their reality out with various incentives that really doesn't coincide with the realistic aspect of their reality – it allows them to keep pushing. A lot of the youngsters don't let go of their fascinations and fantasies, so they pre-occupy their time by writing a rap or trying to put up this imaginary façade of being this strong thug, when in all actuality they are bewildered lost over-grown kids fronting to hide their pain. It's a lot easier to hide their despondency than to allow other prisoners to detect that this prison time is tearing them to pieces inside. Each prisoner has their own reason for living, and whether the reason coincides for a righteous purpose, or not – each person is their own individual reflection.

Every day someone is having a dispute, debate, or an argument about something that's not even meaningful to contemplate a discussion, talkless of actually discussing it. In prison, it's the norm to be surrounded by fake wannabe lawyers, doctors, philosophers, religious dictators and self-proclaimed prophets. It's outright ridiculous what delusional people become in prison and to the extent they would go to prove that what they're professing has validity or veracity to it. Even being standoffish and antisocial, you can still hear those asinine discussions and debates in which sometimes a heated frivolous debate can escalate to a fray until you hear it for yourself, you wouldn't believe the type of arguments that occur in here where realism and relativism are abstract to their reality. It's truly pathetic how single-minded people are in here, and if you spend your mental energy focusing on the nonsensical things that are occurring around you on a daily basis, you'll inevitably stagnate as well. As ridiculous as this may sound, some prisoners will use their imagination as the sole purpose of dealing with their reality, and it's unfathomable for them to try to understand life for what it really is opposed to and what they delude it to be.

Religion is an influential source of a consolidation and uniformity in prison, and some prisoners use religion as a platform to conceal who they really are. There are prisoners who take their religion very, and they've made conversions and transformations to cleanse the unrighteous dirt off their feet from getting high, inebriating, lying, and ever hurting people. The problem with most people in the world especially prisoners, they lack the necessary discipline and self-restraint to be righteous when the test of temptation place a stronghold or a yoke on them while they're physically free to do as they please without the restrictions of a prison gate engulfing them. It's easier said than done when the temptation is not placed upon you or inaccessible to you, and this devoid of discipline is the causative effect of so many recidivists. Of course, not all prisoners are as dangerous as the public would want people to believe because not all criminals are violent offenders or prone to violence. Some criminals in the free-world go to their temple of faith every week, and they struggle with their conscience based on the fact that they're breaking the law; however, they justifiably intellectualize their criminal act by rationalization of them providing for their families. Of course, it doesn't make it right, but the truth of the matter is, there are criminals in the government, in the corporate business and organizations, in the religious groups in the world and every organization you can possibly think of besides those organization who truly fears God.

Some prisoners' mental stability and balance can fluctuate so rapidly that one would have to question whether or not if it's of sound mind to release certain prisoners out of the cage or back into the society. Stability in prison is based on individuality to yen for the zen, and sometimes it's difficult to differentiate from what can be characterized as adjusting opposes to stabilizing one's self. A man's temperament can flux based on the environment, and even when you try to have a peaceful state of mind, something chaotic can occur at any given second, which could rupture your fundamental infrastructure of serenity. Most prisoners whether they know it or not, they've become psychologically dependent upon their prison comrades to help them cope, vent, or channel their aggravation and so forth. This is precisely why prisoners are likely to request to be transferred upon their annual review to a prison where their fellow comrades are located at. It's imperative to be self-reliant considering at any given second you could be separated from the person you've developed a bond with, and that has helped you maintain your mental stability.

At one time, there was unity amongst the prisoners, and they fought for their rights and for the accessibility of books that could essentially help prisoners with their litigation pursuits and educational pursuits. This digital millennium generation has redefined the solidarity of unity and majority of them are misled to believe that joining a gang is part of the movement of unification. Certain gangs have this indoctrination in pursuant to thriving cohesively and stand firmly for justice, equality and liberty, but that's just an illusion because most gang members can barely read. How can any organization collectively form any synergy that's governed by principles if the members are illiterate and ambivalent with undeveloped personality traits. You will commonly hear the gang leaders profess that their organization is a movement to uplift the people and pose opposition to the oppressor, but when you inquire about the brutal mayhem of rivalries and innocent victims – there's a silence amongst the leaders. The blind has been leading the blind for centuries, and the tyranny of the leadership has destroyed cities and nations. There's no righteous unity with honor on this American soil with the respect of the secular organizations, and more importantly, the very fabric of loyalty in the bloodstream has tarnished and diminished dramatically.

In this microwave, digital and millennium generation, most of the young black men were raised without a father because their fathers were either incarcerated, addicted to drugs or dead. Sadly to say, the lack of guardianship can play a major role in the stabling factor of the household. Without having your biological parent in your life, you could develop a gap in your heart, and this gap could represent an emotional void that can hinder you in some way or another. Emotional voids can affect the long-term stability of our life, and if we don't learn how to deal with our voids effectively very early on in life, we're going to go through a lot of ups and downs. A gap in your heart will affect how we view life, how we treat and interact with people and how we cope with the reality of facing obstacles, barriers, trials, and tribulations. Voids can lead to negative fulfilments and positive unfulfillment because people will try to fill their voids by either using drugs, negatively channeling their anger or being licentious as a way to use sexual pleasures to cope with the emotionalism of their problems. Of course, alcoholism is intertwined with this as well. A void in a young black man's heart in the ghetto especially could lead him to death or prison because of the likelihood of the path he'll take within the realms of his dysfunctional environment.

II

Prison can be the physical hell for the dead souls and each day you breathe to sustain your life, you add oxygen to your bones only to eventually be burnt to dust, and that is if you don't allow God to come into your heart. A long-term prison sentence can make you lose your sanity, and you can become a deranged schizoid in which the prison society becomes your imaginary sanctuary or more like your dystopia. A lot of prisoners become accustomed to living their life in prison, and they just live on until they become a decrepit old man and die. Most people would infer that you really don't have any other choice but to learn and accept the reality and conform it. I strongly disagree with this downtrodden defeated ideology because you can be alive grappling in the physical realms but overjoyed and spiritual afloat in the spiritual realms. God can give you an inner-peace that no one can steal from you. The one reality we as humans have to accept is life after death because we're only on this wretched planet for a short period and we will be dead a lot longer than we're alive. Prison is a depressing environment, living in this environment will either bring you closer to God or closer to the devil, and unfortunately, there are only a selective few who will truly find salvation. Being alive or dead is based on your spiritual being — not where you're physically placed at.

In prison, you'll literally watch your hair fall-out by the strand, and you'll see the aging process of each wrinkle on your face as the years pass by with your hair getting thinner and grayer with the seasons. The idle time will exponentially increase your awareness introspectively, and you'll learn things about yourself that you never knew. Idle time can lead to a psychological aberration, or it can lead you to God of a spiritual elevation. I've literally watched a person's hair go completely gray in a three year period before he could reach the age of 33 years. It's not difficult for stress to debacle you as the adversarial enemy to prevail over the battle of the very essence of your existence. When you consider all the negative effects of being in prison — one would think that it would be foolish to risk and jeopardize your freedom for your greed, for your addictions and for any unlawful desires. In this day and age, if you have to spend the rest of your natural life in prison or a considerable amount of years, it's like breathing in toxic gases hoping your lungs can withstand the toxicity of the chemicals you are breathing in. Without a question of a doubt, some people deserve to be in prison for the rest of their natural life because they are flagitiously unconscionable to be able to co-exist amongst people of sound mind or even to co-habit with a cell mate. Some people live like criminal savages, and their savagery must be contained to ensure people that harmony, and their peace is conceivably plausible.

Being in prison can definitely take a psychological toll on you as well as your family. No one really wants to be separated from their family members especially the ones they truly love because it's emotionally unhealthy. No one wants to see their loved ones die in prison but on the flip side, if you murder someone's family member — their families wouldn't mind if you had to suffer and die in prison. Your family support is paramount in here, and some of us are able to remain mentally intact because of the love and support that we receive from the outside. Personally, I don't feel comfortable being burdensome to my family and I try not to put any weight on their shoulders because I'm in tune with the reality of living my life while incarcerated in which I exercise discipline and consideration for those who I love.

Of course, a lot of prisoners don't live by the same beliefs or share my sentiments. Truth be told, most prisoners encumber their families with all their problems as if it's their families fault that they're locked up.

I've watched a lot of prisoners burn their supportive bridges down with their families to the point that their families won't write, accept their calls or even visit them anymore. Usually, prisoners burn their bridges by lying to their family members and using them for money to pay for their drug addictions or gambling addictions. It's a shame how some prisoners have loving, supportive family members and they use and disgracefully exploit them. I'm not perfect obviously, but I have a strong belief system of integrity and principles that I adhere to, and that's punctuated by not abusing or taking for granted of the blessing I receive. I have enough dignity and scruples for those who I love, in which it's unthinkable to play on their conscience like a parasitic knave for my own hidden agenda. Karma cannot be overlooked, and when you mistreat people with duplicity and connivance, you will inevitably reap what you sow.

Prison will take the risibility out of your body, and you will debilitatingly lose the urge to laugh or smile. There's nothing funny about being in prison while being separated from your children and your family, but of course, you have some prisoners who think being in prison is a joke or some type of circus. Prison will definitely wear you out of that surrealistic dream of thinking you're above the law. For centuries, there have been men who thought they were above the laws of the land, but of course, the penalties were quite harsh centuries ago, as death was inevitably the retributive repercussion for an act of unlawfulness. Murder should never be overlooked without punishment unless it was done by self-defense. No one should spend the rest of their natural life in prison unless the crime warrants that determination based on the evidentiary facts of the surrounding circumstances of any criminal case. The laws are becoming outrageous with the amount of time the judges are sentencing people to and not to declare a race card to make a point, but the blacks are receiving more time for the same crime as the whites are receiving. It's understandable how people and politicians are getting utterly fed up with criminals in general; however, there must be fair justice in a nation that strongly prescribes and believes in the constitutionality of fairness, equality, and justice as a way of life.

Life in prison is an awakening experience, and unfortunately, life has a way of revealing things to you in stages and chapters of your pain, disappointments, and setbacks. Some of us are required to feel the fire in the furnace practically to pulverize or cauterize our skin to the bone before we realize a hard head makes a soft ass. When you're young, naïve and foolish, you don't realize the gravity of the seriousness of the consequence of your actions when stealing drugs, carrying around guns and using drugs. I'm certainly not suggesting a young person shouldn't be held accountable for breaking the laws — I'm simply stating that the younger generations don't realize their entire life can be a ruin in a blink of an eye from their youthful foolish indiscretions. A young person is unaware that prison numbs your spine to the point that you sometimes feel like you're an incapacitated paraplegic mute. There will be days when you don't want to talk or even move your body because your reality starts digging holes into your mind and bones, while your heart is suffocating. Some of these young fools in prison have the tendency to play around like a winsome frolicsome puppy at a playground, but all the playing gradually stops over the years especially when people move on with their lives or start to depart from this planet. All the playing stops when the support from your family starts to diminish, dwindle and diminish, or when you truly have your epiphanous awakening and your reality hits so hard it knocks you off your feet. Once you realize your life is being wasted away in a prison cell and the world is moving ahead – one would have to ask themselves "is this what I was placed on this earth for?"

The Virginia prison system has implemented new micro-management policies and procedures wherefore the administrators at the main headquarter are conveying to the prison wardens to do whatever is necessary as an inducement or disincentive to minimize disruptive or assaultive behavior. Virginia has built these unnecessary supermaximum prisons as a psychological deterrence to get offenders to comply with the rules and regulations, in which they conduct annual assessment report to determine your security placement and good time earning. One disciplinary infraction that doesn't even involves a weapon, an assault or a gang-related incident, the prison administration can have you transferred to a supermaximum prison. The Virginia prison system waste millions of tax payer's money on gas alone for transferring prisoners around simply to control the psychodynamics of prisoners minds. The prison system is setup whereas you're accommodated with certain privileges when you are transferred to a lower custody prison if you abide by the treatment recommendation that they set forth. Each prisoner must be programmatic and maintain good conduct with productiveness in order to receive good reviews for a counselor's recommendations during the annual review. If your progress is deemed unsatisfactory, your transfer will be denied for a lower custody and possibly approved for a higher security custody transfer. Normally, at any other prison systems, if you become disruptive or engage in a physical altercation, you'll face isolation time in segregation at worst but the Virginia prison system has strict ramifications; one infraction could be reprehensible in denying you a transfer to a lower custody security prison and more importantly that same minor offense could be the reason why the parole board denies you of parole. The prison system has a point scale system that allows the prison administration to tabulate the points to determine if you meet the criteria's to be transferred to lower or higher security prison. The points system are quantified on the basis of your age, the length of your sentence, your crime, your priors, your educational status, your conduct status and your prison employment status. You can receive deductible points when you remain infraction free and comply with your annual treatment plans. Depending on the severity of the last disciplinary offense – one year of remaining charge free will not constitute a favorable security transfer. Certain offenses require a 24 month period of infraction-free in order to meet the requirements to be transferred. Of course, all the will be deducted, assessed and computed to determine the rationale of a counselors recommendations.

A G.ED. is the extent of what D.O.C. will offer for your education, and if you want to further your education by taking some college courses, you would have to pay with your own money. All grants to my knowledge have been terminated, and of course, D.O.C will not give you any assistance in helping you to further your education. There's really no trades you can take that would help you find a job in the streets except the H-VAC program, in which the waiting list is interminable by the time you get in the class – that's if you even get in which takes about 18 months to get in and about 18 months to complete it. Most of the time, the prisoners are not in the particular prison that they initially started the program wherefore you will be transferred before you can complete the program. The basic Vocational classes most prison's offer is custodian maintenance and dry-wall classes. In order to get in barber school, you would practically have to be a non-violent offender at a very low custody prison; however, there are exceptions if you're fortunate to get to a prison that offers those programs because no high-security prison offer certain vocational programs, in terms of H-VAC or barber school. Once you receive your G.E.D., all you can truly do is read books to self-educate yourself unless you have family members who can pay for the tuition fees of a correspondence college course.

In prison, pride travels through the air and damn near where everyone has a defensive mechanism in which most prisoner's try so hard to conceal their true identity and feelings about being incarcerated and how it's affecting them detrimentally. A lot of gang member especially clings to one another for emotional support coupled with an objectified movement of unity as they would like to believe. In all actuality, the majority of the gang members have an ulterior motive to join a gang and whether it's for protection, compensatory privileges or any other benefits that come with joining a gang – it's still counterproductive. The irony of joining a gang for all the wrong reasons is that eventually, the light will be shed to illuminate the truth that being a gang member has nothing to do with the uplifting of the oppressor. Gangs are criminal organizations acting in the capacity of synergy and trying to emulate the Italian's infamous criminal infrastructure, but the only problem is, the leadership is compromised, and the foundation is in disarray with consorted infiltrators. Most of the time, the so-called foot soldiers are considered to be collateral damages in the Virginia system, in which they're ordered to execute foolish demonstrative acts of assault, robbery or whatever is required in order for the leaders actualize their agendas. Gang leader's ideology is demagogic in respect to feeding their foot soldiers and even their ranking soldiers with this illusion that the more work they put, it's less likely for them to climb the ranks in an accelerating fashion. The expression of putting "work-in" simply means carrying out any task you fulfill which is normally associated with a negative illustration.

There are a lot of talented individuals in prison, and it's amazing the sort of ingenious creativity and ingenuity they have. I've seen prisoners make classic cars out of soap and their designs are impeccable with a precision that is truly impressive. I've seen an artist who drew all the presidents in these incredible miniature portraits, and you would be astoundingly amazed how identical the portraits were. I've seen prisoners burn plastic spoons and form an animal of all sorts, in which the most exquisite animal I've seen molded with plastic spoons was a lion, and you wouldn't believe it unless you saw it. There are talented poets and writers in here, and it's unfortunate how so much talent is being wasted away in a prison cell. Prisoners make chains, rugs, hats and anything else you can think of with an artistic approach with self-made tools that are characterized as contraband. Any person would be flabbergasted how you could take a paper clip and use it as a tool to make all sorts of things. Without a question of a doubt, idle time or available time, enable prisoners to try come up with ingenious ideas to make creative things because after all, their talent becomes their hustle in here. The most renown scientists, engineers, and architects are perplexed by the extraordinary examples of what ancient people were able to build monolithically with the very unsophisticated tools but the one immutable fact people keep omitting ;ancient people use the element of time to tap into their most creative source of impulse, in which time, mental energy and unrelenting determination was the compelling factor to achieve unimaginable things in the ancient vintage.

Nothing is free in prison. Even a conversation can cost you a petty value of soup, which is better known as oodles noodles soup. An indigent prisoner can hold a conversation with you to give you time to vent or kill some time with the conversation only to objectively be waiting for the right opportunity to ask you for soup. The dynamics in prison is synonymous to the free world because drugs, portraits, drawings, tattoos and everything else cost in here, even though the business transactions are on a very small scale of a profit. In prison, a dollar is equivalent to five dollars on the streets. Five dollars in prison can get you stabbed if you try to take advantage of someone's earning or refuse to pay the bill you owe.

If you're a prisoner with the means to buy what you want, it seems like everyone gravitates to you in an ingratiating way as if they're your best friend. A prisoner who's acknowledged for having here is a prisoner who gets a lot of unnecessary attention they're a high caliber of a thorough-bred; meaning, a man who doesn't back down from anyone and don't tolerate any disrespect. Usually, everything is motivated by an ulterior motive in prison, and ninety percent of the prisoners are trying to con or manipulate someone out of something. It's difficult to accept anyone as a genuine person in an environment where credibility, trust, and sincerity are almost oblivious. Regardless of how righteous we appear to others, we are still criminals, and most of us still have the criminal mentality that a dollar to gain is a dollar to make. You can't have any expectations for someone to deal with principles in here because it's quite obvious what you're surrounded by. There are a selective few who have dignified integrity, scruples but you may not encounter with that type of individual for years at a time, and that's only if you two are fortunate to meet one another. Don't misconstrue my words, you have a lot of prisoners who fundamentally deal with basic principles but when you exceed the parameters of basically; I would suggest to anyone to be dubious about a person, unless you've known a person for years and more importantly you've had an extensive history of dealing or conducting business with them. Conducting transactions with people involving money has a way of revealing people for who they are, as opposed to what they project to be. You don't know a person until money is in the equation.

Being antisocial or standoffish can essentially keep you away from a lot of foolishness, but the downside is the monotonous effect it will have on you in the rit of doing your time. It's not healthy to be utterly socially withdrawn, but with the caliber of individuals you're surrounded by, you don't have a lot of options unless you want to be a part of the ostensive phoniness that the other prisoners personify. I prefer to be a recluse than to subject myself to the demoralizing standards of being an unscrupulous heathen. The boredom and the banality are unquestionably overwhelming, but I would rather be overwhelmed than to be uncharacteristically phony. Sometimes the days are longer when you're not playing tabletops games or socializing, but that comes with the territory of staying at a distance from interactions. Three days out of a week seem like a dejavu, and as much as you try to change your routine around the everyday cycle can be seen routinized. The continuity of time is enveloped by your will to use it wisely or waste it unwisely. Invariably, time can be your worst enemy or time can be your salvation and deliverance. Time in prison can be interminably oppressive especially if you're a captive in the spiritual and emotional realms of your mind and spirit. Empty time with isolation can create a fascinating but almost an eccentric imagination, and if your mind uses your imagination as a platform to cope, eventually the figment of your imagination will distort your reality. Empty or idle time can be perilous, in the sense of allowing the time to plague your thoughts with destructive ideations of despair. Isolation can make you go haywire if you don't consciously keep your sanity intact to stay afloat.

A prison is a place I could never acclimatize myself, and it's a physical hell that can tear your heart to pieces if you have a conscience to want to change. It's a mindboggling experience either way,some people would prefer to live in this misery with their perverse criminal mentalities for the rest of their natural life but with me, I would rather die and see Jesus if I'm not able to get another opportunity to restore my tainted youthful indiscretions that ultimately led me to prison. I want to be able to show that I can live a legitimate life and destigmatize the status quo involving the recidivism. The most important aspect of redeeming myself is showing those who I love that I can achieve things in the world by learning to love God more, myself and my family to the point I would dispel all inner-demons by never risking or jeopardizing my freedom again. I would rather strengthen my walk in faith as I gradually renew my mind before I would be inclined to focus on being released.

The new arrivals are coming into the system younger and younger, and you can see the transparency of the pain in their eyes as if this new world has already shattered their hope for survival. This new world I'm referring to is the prison society that they just enter. A lot of those youngsters act like they were tough on the streets with their pistols, but most of them come to prison scared to death. Of course you can't be fooled by their youthful, innocent faces because those same innocent faces were capable of such unspeakable violent acts; moreover, people, generally have this idea of a depiction of what a killer may look like. Murderers can blend with people with the normalcy of being employed, attending social gatherings, and even attending church. It's not wise to categorically characterize a person based with people with the normalcy of being employed, attending social gatherings, and even attending church, or categorically characterize a person based on the external features of their demeanor, disposition or attitude. I've seen likable, and society friendly people murder their own best friends, even weep, and bemoan at the funeral while being the pall-bearer. The irony of this particular incident, the mother nor did anyone else suspect this person was involved with the murder of his own best friend in which the culprit had this ingenuous appearance about him.

In this day and time, youngsters are sometimes pressured to commit violent acts because, in the ghettos, it's very territorial to the point that there are deadly frays of rivalry quarrels between neighborhoods that consequently lead to adversarial societal carnage and collateral casualties. In some cases, people don't have an alternative option but to retaliate because a retaliatory response could essentiality save your life or even cost you your life. I'm certainly not suggesting retaliatory response could essentially save your life or even cost you your life, neither do I suggest retaliation is the methodology to handle certain situations; however, I am implying that some of us are at war and self-preservation for survival is imperative. Unfortunately, in certain instances, the reality of war tactics to survive requires a swift fatal response, and regardless if it's in the ghettos or Iran, the common denominator is; Survival. I'm certainly not trying to pontificate the surviving should be by one's discretion because there are laws that must be adhered to. Peer pressure is very serious in the ghettos because if you're perceived as being a weak person, no one will respect, then you can become a prospective candidate for the predators to pick at you like a vulture picks at a dead caucus. Of course, you will always have someone that's an inexperienced self-proclaimed intellectual who will disagree with these dynamics of the ghettos. It's always a person who will profess that they have been through the hardships of being raised in the ghettos punctuated by the adversities; however, they've successfully got out of the ghettos with a well-accomplished career. There aren't any arguably excuses to be made because you have people in the ghettos who are honor roll students, trying to make something of their life, and they still get murdered innocently. Life is like rolling a dice sometimes, but with God, you can't go wrong. There will be pessimists and naysayers who will declare that people are simply making excuses to justifiably explain their reality just for the sake of justification as to why they committed deadly violent crimes. In a lot of cases, it's not an excuse; It's the truth. If you never lived in the ghettos where murder and violence is a normal occurrence, you really shouldn't refute or speak on what the lifestyle is like and how the environment plays a tremendous role in who you become. Undeniably you have very successful people that we raised in the ghettos, but it's one thing to live in a ghetto, and it's a total differentiation to be entrenched in the ghettos, you automatically sign up for everything that comes with the prescription. It's almost as if you're subscribing to this way of life because once you get the exposure and experience wherefore as pathetic as this may sound, it can become intoxicating. Living in the ghettos or being raised in the ghetto is one dimension; however, being bred to the streets of the ghetto is not tantamount to the first contextualize equation. The odds of being successful after being bred to the streets of the ghettos is disproportionally staggering to the statistics.

In prison, you can learn to hate living, you can learn to accept the reality of what life is really about, or you can even learn to come to terms with the inevitability of your fate and your destiny. Of course, there are a lot of others things you can learn but that all depends on what state or frame of mind you are in when the opportunity presents itself for you to learn something. It's ridiculous how so many prisoners just sit around waiting for someone to teach them something oppose to taking the initiative to study, read, research, pray, meditate and educate themselves. You can't force anyone to learn, you certainly can't force anyone to change, and if a person chooses to be complacently illiterate or ignorant because they lack the necessary discipline, drive, and patience; that's their choice. If a person wants to remain stagnant and stationary in their bewilderment, then that's their choice as well. Television is one of the main distractions, and if prisoners spend half of the time or even a fraction of their time that they spend watching T.V. to read a book, they would be able to see some progress in the intellectual spectrum. In the 70's, practically everyone read books and magazines in the prison system because there weren't televisions in the cells and even if they didn't read on a regular basis, they at least attempted to read something. Of course, I wasn't in the prison system in the 70's or 80's because that was before my time obviously but I've thoroughly done my research, and I've been around prison veterans of that vintage who currently are still incarcerated.

Every prisoner has their perspective about being incarcerated, and of course, some of their views are diametrically contrarious to their reality because they're simply delusional as hell; however, the reality is, after a while anyone would start to yearn for something different after watching your years pass you by. You have a lot of veteran convicts who are still going around speaking about this hogwash of a revolution and how the white man is the oppressor and so-forth. Those same convicts who are speaking negatively about the white man being the blue-eyed devil, are the same ones who will break their necks to try and get a young white and try to turn him to a personal sex slave. The hypocrisy is so outrageous that you would easily stop having discussions with other prisoners who say one thing and do the exact opposite. It's a common thing to see and hear a bunch of hypocrites talk about politics and religion. It's a whole lot of purveying of "inmate.com" prison gossip and politics. The contradiction is overwhelming because it's a constant observation of nosy prisoners who are either intrusive with prying or probing, or too immersed with focalizing on what the next prisoner is doing.

People, in general, don't have the time nor energy to try to distinguish if a criminal can be reformed or not, even a trial judge doesn't bother to consider the rehabilitating factors either, especially when it comes to imposing a sentence. Law abiding citizens don't like the idea of being amongst ex-convicts because of the stigma of the ex-con's unpredictability of possibly regressing to committing another crime. People don't feel safe living adjacent to ex-offenders because it's always a doubt of fear and trepidation of the potentiality of a dangerous person being triggered. Fear can make people qualm, and it's a debilitating apprehension in which it can cause acute anxiety issues, especially if a person never had any experience of violence. The immutable fact is, once you're besmirched with a criminal record, your credibility is shattered from the perspective of the average law-abiding citizen. Fear has always been a factor in deterring people from embracing anyone because how can you trust someone you fear. No one likes to be placed in a situation where they have to look over their shoulders or walk on eggshells in this quandary state of mind. A criminal can post-traumatically cause psychological problems, whereas a person could harness antipathy against a particular criminal or all criminals the rest of their lives. Criminals are a vexation to some people's spirits, and every time they hear or see the media sensationalize a criminal act with the galvanize publicity, this process will only exacerbate the instilled fear and trauma.

People would agree that criminals and terrorist make life more complicated and miserable than it needs to be and sadly to say, hateful feelings of resentment is how people cope and deal with their pain and bereavement. There's nothing you can say to people who have suffered from the victimization of a criminal when you're a criminal yourself. Generally, people of sound mind like to embrace love, harmony, and peace, and when there are people who enjoy disharmony and war, you can't co-exist together. People who believe in a system of love would naturally prefer not to be near criminals. Moreover, they probably would prefer that most criminals be ostracized, alienated or exiled from the land upon which they live. An Asian-American who was mentally disturbed shot and murdered 32 innocent people and the devastation of that massacre sent a shock-wave of sadness throughout the country. That's a prime example of why so many people have developed a strong abhorrence against criminals, and that's why people are unsympathetic towards first-time offenders that are normally relatively young underprivileged minorities.

The perception of criminals has changed over the years because the social media is exposing the unspeakable crimes from every corner of the planet, in which the grotesque of the mayhem has always been capsuled for political and social agendas. There was a juncture when it was unheard of for a heinous act to be committed in certain urban areas, but now, even the suburbs are being directly affected by this dissemination of violence. Most people didn't care if brutality and mayhem remained in the realms of the ghettos but once criminals started spreading their violence abroad, then comes the negative publicity of hysteria. It's almost as if politicians feel compelled to set an example by extending mandatory sentencing guideline and finding the necessary funds to build more prisons to house more prisoners. People can be unfair and evil to others, and that is the evolutionary aspect of our existence in which even evil can evolve.

Prison is a poisonous reptilian environment, and it feels like prison travels through the air, in which you're being contaminated by the toxicity in the airwaves. You would think death has to be better than this because it's like you're suffocating on your oxygen. Even your heart can gradually deteriorate through the decadence of these interminable dreary years. One would think that once you repent by cleansing your heart and mind of the impurities that ultimately led you to prison, you would be able to offer some help as a token of your redemption and contribution; however, it seems implausible to contribute to anything in prison. Of course, not all of us in prison is evil dissolute fools, but it doesn't make any difference to anyone except your family, because the society has marked you off as if you're the devil's servant. Trying to destigmatize the status quo while being incarcerated behind the prison walls, would be virtually impractical; however, this shouldn't be one's focus while incarcerated and furthermore the primary focus should always be to learn more about God.

Each day I hear about the calamities and atrocities that are occurring throughout the world, and sometimes I feel utterly melancholic because it's as if I'm categorically a part of those dehumanizing evildoers. I haven't murdered, raped or terrorized anyone but I'm sure I've placed trauma into the victim's heart, and that alone makes me feel like I was a part of the evil that circulates in the world. It's easy to declare that evil is a part of living justifiably but I would never accept that as a part of living to connote that it's the natural way of our existence. People allow evil to exist and even though there will always be evil within this world, we should never accept or conform to this as a part of living. Living coincides with our volition and how we make it be, but unfortunately, people try to dictate other people's lives with their tyranny and demagogic evil. Self-righteous and hypocritical people will try to spread their philosophical views on life to perpetuate the continuity of their evil and hidden agendas. The prison was built to contain a certain amount of evil, and quite naturally too many evil entities together can cause a seismic tidal wave of evil, which is practically unavoidable not to feel the satanic effect.

Prison can make you delusional and exceedingly paranoid, to the point you'll question yourself as to who you're becoming. I'm not solely speaking on the type of paranoia that's associated with fear and apprehension of the people you're surrounded by, but I'm also referring to the sort of paranoia in which you become hallucinatory. In prison, you have a lot of time for introspection, and you'll analyze things that you would have probably never thought about before your imprisonment. Undoubtedly, you can lose your sanity and begin to go haywire in which stress and depression can eat you up so badly that you become a dead soul waiting to succumb. The prison at one point in time could preserve you and could have a salubrious effect on the conditions of your physical health because exercising become a part of your daily routine and the food complied with the dietary health standards. I believe this vintage of the prison system serving healthy foods were in the course of the late 80s till about the millennium, but after that juncture, the food became inadequate and unhealthy therefore your body, skin and health aren't preserved as much.

Each day you deal with the burden of not knowing what's in store for your future and every day you're burdened by the oxygen, and your body inhales because of the dreariness of your spirits, which has your mind and heart crest-fallen. Death is inevitable of course but what's life without a purposeful cause and why should prison be the last chapter of our life. How do you live amongst so much evil that your good spirits are buried, in which no one can see or identify with you beneath the evil that makes you unrecognizable as an entry that can help people? Trying to swim in the water with sharks with a humble tone will make you come up for air like an amphibian because it can be exhaustive to maintain your composure and restraint. Cold blooded sharks don't co-exist well with amphibious types of people because metaphorically it's as if you're trying to blend salt in an open wound. If you were once an animal, in which you exhibit animalistic traits, trying to normalize yourself with human qualities is a process, but the decision must be made to think like a conscientious human or an apathetic animal.

There's a common acceptance of ignorance in prison, and usually, prisoners are more receptive to hear from a narrow-minded, ignorant person whose view is outright unrealistically pathetic. Every day there's a debate or argument about something frivolous that you wouldn't even contemplate or gestate the thought to entertain these absurd discussions. Just like in the free-world, religion, and politics is a common discussion amongst the rare ones who do read, but for the other prisoners, their discussions are about rap, fashion trends, sports, criminal endeavors and current crimes that are being committed. In prison, you have all sorts of imaginary lawyers, dictators, and philosophers and some are simply delusional whereas they think they meet the qualification of having a voice to speak on that particular profession. I'm certainly not trying to undermine or imply that people's voices in prison shouldn't be relevant because there is a great deal of potential in prison; however, I'm specifically referring to the degenerate hypocrites that say one thing but illustrates the epitome of hypocrisy. There are prisoners who've spent a considerable amount of their time and energy researching and reading caseloads studiously. Some prisoners have studied the law for so long that they can properly file any petition as if it was done at a law firm, and of course, that's not the extent of their capabilities. There are some very intelligent talented people in prison, but unfortunately, most of them are recidivists that seem to only cultivate their talent when they get locked back up.

Time flies by in prison if you keep your mind occupied; however, time can go very slow whereas it seems like one day is equivalent to three days. The boredom in prison can drive you crazy if you don't try to keep yourself busy. Idle time can have a deleterious effect on you if you utilize your time wisely because you can easily get caught up in the reminiscent stress of what ultimately led you to prison and the memory lane of what occurred in your life. If you have a lengthy sentence, you'll have enough time to reminisce things you've forgotten about, and you remember insignificant details of certain events of your life that you wouldn't even have thought about if you were free. In prison, everything in retrospect will surface and resurface to the point that you will watch your life like a movie in your head. I think I'm a very nostalgic individual and I've practically stored most of my childhood memories, and I have harbored ill-will feelings about certain ordeals I've endured. Sometimes it can be psychologically unhealthy for anyone to resurface old memories because most of us humans have a different time letting go of our past and if our past precludes us from excelling, then we have to create our future. It's not simple to forget certain aspects of our past, but we can bury it in our thoughts and learn to forgive whomever, to move on to the next chapter of our life.

Prison makes it hard to even have any chapter in your life because there are no relevant changes besides the fact that you're getting older and you may lose someone you love behind these gates in a prison cell. You can become more mature and to some degree but that's the only extent of what may change in your life without God. You can certainly learn new things by reading books, but throughout these maturation stages of growth in many areas, you still will be confined to the realms of this prison world. Opening and closing a chapter in your life will be based on the books you've read to acquire a certain amount of education and knowledge; however God created your book of life, and through him comes wisdom, the key element to life. Some people have wisdom and don't even apply it in certain instances, it's as if without faith in God, knowledge, wisdom, and understanding are all synonymous to adjectives with a fruitless, useless meaning. Once you enter this pit of captivity, you will not be privileged to have found favorable memories of enjoying yourself with those who you love unless it's memories of the past. In hindsight, it changes the equation but if you weigh everything on the scale, and you weigh in everything you'll lose, only a fool would decide to continue to risk their freedom with the pursuit of their criminal endeavors.

A man has to rehabilitate himself, and if he doesn't believe in God, he would have to come to terms with the fact that he has to guide himself to his salvation. The journey is going to be rough either way, but if you don't believe in God, you're already spiritually dead, and the devil will have a field day with sabotaging and crippling you every time the opportunity is available. Of course, the devil will target you if he feels you're getting closer to God and he will prevail in his mission if you're not steadfastly firm in rebuking Satan. I'm not a religious person, but I believe in God, and I've conclusively determined that the devil is too powerful for any human to try to fight or defend against him without God's guidance and armor on. Without God, there's no rehabilitation because God holds the profound keys and tools for us to unlock certain doors in the geography of our minds and spirits to be renewed and transformed. As much as some people would profess that I'm talking out of the side of my head, this is something we will all eventually see for ourselves. As prisoners, we've already gambled with our physical freedom. The question is; do we want to gamble with our spiritual freedom as well.

Most of us know the confinement of prisons are imperative for our societal coexistence and as I previously mentioned – prison is a society in itself but do we agree that there must be evil to ensure the ecological balance of evils vs good scenario. Of course, most of us will probably question why God allows certain tragedies to occur and my guess would be, what would life be, without the pain, joy, suffering, happiness, and death? Of course, I don't agree with people's choices to sabotage, ruin, and destroy other people's lives and I wish I could do something to apply my role in helping people, but I know and understand the constraints that are stigmatically placed on me coincide with the restrictions of being incarcerated. I've been unbalanced, unstable and prone to aggression since I was very young and sadly to say, the mental anguish, pain and emotional trauma of scars that were inflicted on me, made my heart evil, in which I felt comfortable with the idea of people dying and suffering. I never thought my heart would change because my mind and heart poisoned with the defilement of the street life as if I had venom flowing through my bloodstream. I always knew or felt like something was different about me when I hung around a certain individual who would kill people in the streets for senseless reasons. I mean they weren't killing 9 to 5 law abiding citizens – they were killing people who signed up for the codes of the street. I felt out of place deep down inside I was longing for guidance to help me flush out the evilness in my bloodstream. My environment and my peers had shackles on me whereas everything about my life was too dysfunctional and unstable to pull me away from the prison I was sucking on. Early death for me was almost inevitable, but I was spared, of course, it was a blessing, but I would be lying if I was to say I didn't doubt whether or not I was worthy for this blessing.

Each day in prison you wake up, and it's your choice to live to see another day or die and end your misery. Every man has his breaking point, and prison can place you at the edge of the cliff of a mountain. Most prisoners will not divulge their Achilles-heel because men don't like to be exposed of the underbelly section of their minds and they don't like to admit that this prison time is taking a toll on them. I can see the dejection in their eyes when they come back from their visitations or when they get off the phone with their relatives. As much as they would like to believe their pain is undetected by this tough-man façade they put up, I'm able to see through their camouflaged dissemblance. I've been told that I'm quite analytical in which I practically smell pain and of course I'm facetious, but I can read people pretty well. Pain is not an enjoyable emotion, and the emotional pain of being separated from those you love can eat you up inside like a maggot feeding off a dead caucus. Prison can be a physical hell, but it's your choice to live with it by God's grace and deliverance or die with it hoping death is better than this.

Prison is an environment that will make you a believer, a believer of fate, a believer of destiny or a believer of your demise. A lot of people take life for a joke, and they don't realize how serious life is until they face an eye awakening experience. Prison is an eye awakening experience; however most of the time it will take some years for people to realize the seriousness of their imprisonment. Unfortunately, with some people, it would take them to lose someone that's close to their hearts before they begin to understand the gravity of life while residing behind a prison cell while you lose your loved ones. It's sad how it most results to that sort of tragedy before some people open their eyes to their reality to reprogram and recondition their minds and mentality. Prison is not a place for games or infantile frolicking, but some prisoners act as if this is some form of a retreat or a vacation to have fun and enjoy themselves.

When you have a lot of time over your head, you can't be wasting your time playing around as if this is a joke and the sooner you realize how serious your life is, the sooner you can begin your journey if searching for salvation.

In prison, it's bad enough that you have to deal with the guards' antagonism and provocation nevertheless other prisoners nonsense as well. The stress can easily accumulate for which you become like a time bomb ready to implode and explode. If you don't have the willpower to maintain your self-control, this journey will be a rough one, and it could lead you to death. Your situation and your circumstances can become dreadful if you allow your mind to soak into the poison you're surrounded by. You're surrounded by cold-blooded murderers, rapists and child molesters, so you'll feel the negative energy that's enveloped in pure unadulterated evil. The question is can you be around those sort of individuals without allowing their venom to affect you negatively, whether it's being hateful towards them or stagnated by the seemingly dead energy in the air. Unfortunately, most prisoners allow themselves to feed off the energy they're surrounded by, and consequently, they fall into the trap of destruction that poses a detour and a downward spiral of any attempt to change.

A prison guard can make things very uncomfortable for you especially if his rank permits him to do practically anything he wants. In most prisons, you're going to have an outright ass-hole guard who comes to work with a chip on his shoulders, in which he will deliberately go around targeting certain prisoners either by inciting or provoking them to respond or react inappropriately. The instigation of a guard's antagonism can make you utterly violative with assaultive and disruptive behavioral issues and naturally that sort of behavior is dealt with swiftly by disciplinary actions which consist of isolation confinement. In isolation confinement, you lose all your privileges except being able to take a shower and being fed your meals each day. Some guards who are very discriminatory towards criminals – they will use the disciplinary procedures and policies as leverage to provoke you hoping that you would do anything so they can justifiably write you an infraction and even lie if necessary. There are guards who've lost loved ones from criminals, and they come to work every single day with this hateful disposition and demeanor with the intentions to try to vex you to the bone. One particular guard I have an encounter with, his daughter was raped and badly beaten, he bluntly confided in me one day, and he stated that if it was up to him and he could get away with it, he would go to every damn cell and blow every sex offenders brains out. The guard divulged that to me when I inquired about his ill-tempered and irrational ways. After he disclosed that to me, he told me he has never told an inmate before, but it was something about me that was different to him that he couldn't explain.

Every prisoner tries to develop an outlet for themselves because it's like a therapeutic process of being able to do things to keep you aplomb, mentally balanced and emotionally stable. For some prisoner, such as myself, it's unimaginable to be in prison without having someone on this planet who loves me. The love and encouragement from your family can be your oxygen and sanity when in all actuality God is supposed to be your oxygen and sanity. Unfortunately, losing someone you love behind a prison cell can overwhelmingly shatter your heart and cripple your spirits. I've seen people go completely crazy by self-mutilating themselves as an attempt to commit suicide and even commit suicide. Most of us in prison won't be able to traditionally cope with the fact of losing a loved one because being able to attend their funeral while being incarcerated is highly unlikely and that alone can affect the bereavement process. An outlet allows you to channel out things that will enable you to refocus your attention only if it's effective obviously, and it's essentially imperative to create positive reinforcements so the negativity won't influence your judgment skills. Prisoners use drug as an outlet, as a coping mechanism or as a mental escapism and of course this may not lead to a positive outlet to deal with the reality of their imprisonment; however their self-destructive habits and addictions is what led them to prison in the first place and with most cases, just because you're in prison, that doesn't mean the addictions will disappear. Prison obviously make drugs less inaccessible but a friend will figure out a way to get their hands on some drugs, and a hustler will figure out a way to sell it unless either of them is housed at the ADX Federal Super maximum prison.

Everyday, there's some form of tension amongst each other, and we as criminals can be some of the most unpredictable impetuous individuals that you would ever encounter with. You simply don't know what may trigger their explosive tendencies and of course, I'm not excluding myself, but I've learned how to control my impulsivity and aggression for the most part. I can become aggressively inflammatory if I'm affronted by any innuendo or onslaught, in which it can get ugly; however, I'm gradually renewing my mind. Usually, confrontational conflicts occur when competitiveness, ego, pride, hunger or a violation is placed in the equation, whether it's contact sports, gambling or arguments which consists of who's more knowledgeable about a meaningless topic of a discussion. Physical altercations can start with one prisoner starring at another in the wrong way. Once you surpass those foolish pride issues of all that street and prison mentality, you'll become more discreet and wiser not to feed into that nonsense. Certain prison codes amongst the prisoners must be dealt with, or it could negatively impact your survival and peace of mind but of course being a child and a servant of God; It's amazingly phenomenal of the refuge he will give you especially if you're authentic, fearless soldier and sheep as I am to him.

In retrospect, my aggression has always played a role in my setbacks, and as much as I tried to have some self-control, it seemed like I became more uncontrollable to myself with an inner war. My truculence wasn't to the point that I would go around haphazardly hurting people or doing senseless things to people. My mental balance could be destabilized or triggered for which I would exhibit violence if it deems necessary. I wasn't brought up to fear any man nevertheless any potential foe or enemy, and I came to prison with this mentality of having a very low tolerance for any bullshit or disrespect. The first week I arrived at Mecklenburg Correction Center, I searched for a knife, AKA a "shank," and I was able to obtain several knives, and I strategically hid the knives in several locations. I've been fighting all my life based on how I looked and didn't mind fist fighting or doing whatever that was required to defend myself. I knew I had to take a defensive precautionary measure of keeping myself armed because, from my experience in the Maryland prison system and D.C. jail, a shank could swiftly incapacitate you with one blow regardless how skillful you were with your hands when it came to rumbling. I didn't care what the next prisoner was capable of doing because I knew I was capable of doing and I knew if I were slightly disrespected from anyone, I wouldn't hesitate to attack the culprit without giving anyone any preparation of my attack.

The prison violence was nothing new to me because I was raised up in Southeast Washington D.C., where violence was almost indigenous, so I prepared for any physical conflicts that may even turn into a deadly conflict. I spent over 4 years approximately in two supermaximum prisons and over 8 years in a high maximum level 5 prison, and throughout those years, I learned a great deal about myself.

I learned how my aggressive flaws were ultimately precluding me from finding inner-[peace and a balanced spirit and mind. Throughout my journey, I realized how ignorant, complexed, and confounded I was, and once I received my enlightenment, I couldn't believe how I allow so much evil and poison to pollute my mind. I've never been a drug addict, believe it or not; I never liked drugs, I've seen what it did to my father and my late aunt, which she died from AIDS. As much as I didn't like to use drugs, I had no problem selling drugs. The poison I'm referring to is the misguidance, misinformation and the misattribution to the so-called precepts of the streets in which it instilled into my mind. We all go through this susceptible, pliable phase for which we can be receptive to all the abstract negative views and perspectives that are being lodged into our minds.

III

As much as I hate to admit to my reality, if I would have come to prison under these circumstances – I would be either dead or probably have a life-sentence in another prison system. The truth of the matter, the prison has been a blessing, and if you knew me before I was transformed, that statement in itself is remarkable for me o profess out of my mouth. I'm locked up for something that was an accident but regardless how inadvertent it may have been if I hadn't been there, this wouldn't have occurred. I take full responsibility for my actions because my acceptance is key to my spiritual growth and there's no need to try to intellectualize, rationalize, or justifiably actualize my indiscretions as if I'm the victim. I was seventeen years old when this crime occurred, and as much as I would have liked to go back in time to talk to my younger self, we all know that's a figment of our imagination.

Prison is an environment that you'll only see faces of hate, bitterness, despondency, stress, and pain. Happiness doesn't exist in here, but you can gain an indescribable source of inner peace; wherefore God has brought you closer to him to be placed in his bosom to soothe your mind, body, and spirit with your obedience. It's difficult that the people I've met over the years were icy, coldblooded murderers on the streets and unfortunately, most of the people I've allowed in my social circles are genuine brothers who embody good qualities, but they are all murderers. I'm able to see the goodness in their hearts because individually they all are honorably authentic with the display of integrity and principles. One of my strongest associates – border-line from being a friend, he murdered two people, but if you met him, you wouldn't even be able to picture him committing those acts of murder. He was practically a baby when the crimes he committed occurred, he was only 14 years old, but in the judge's eyes, they adjudicated him as an adult. It wasn't his intentions to murder two people, but unfortunately, he did and consequently he may spend over 35 years of his life behind bars. There have been many nights when he has questioned himself remorsefully and broke down in tears for his regrettable sympathy of what occurred. Now some of those tears may be attributed to doing the number of years he has to do for which the notion in itself of his reality is daunting and debilitating. Unfortunately, he's characterized on the chart of the statistical category of being influenced by his older peers, but regardless of whom influenced him, once he murdered someone, he must be punished in accordance to his actions of individual accountability from the perspective of the laws.

A lot of people in the society of abroad don't understand how violence is unavoidable at times in the projects or even elsewhere. You don't have to take the first blow to become a target to be killed; you can be killed just for living in a certain neighborhood. In the ghettos, you can't go to the police because then you'll be labeled as a snitch and this defamatory label can cause you to be killed or possibly one of your family members will be killed if they can't get to you. In the ghettos, your enemy will target your family if they can't get to you and that's the retribution penalty for your flagrant violation of the streets codes; moreover, you will still be a target to be murdered even after your family member becomes a casualty. As much as people would like to believe there's a law to protect you when you defend yourself, that law doesn't apply in the ghettos. If a person pulls out a gun on you and fire at you with intentions to kill you but in return, you fire back and murder that person — in the ghettos the prosecutor will charge you with murder and wouldn't give a damn how many witnesses corroborates your version of self-defense of what happened. This is the reality of living in poverty-stricken areas where there's a liquor store in the proximity of every corner in the radius in all different directions or a drug dealer. People generally don't care about what occurs in the ghetto. If it doesn't reflect on their middle class or suburban neighborhoods, in their point of view why bother to emphasize trying to penetrate the preventative measures to decrease the violence in the ghettos. Politicians will by-pass the bureaucracy to gentrify the impoverished under-privileged neighborhoods, so the consensus is, why waste or invest money into a dilapidated cemetery, in which that's what the ghettos are perceived as regarding a dead zone cemetery. Gentrification is not systematically done to help the families in the ghettos obviously, but of course, political figures and investors thrive off your naivety.

I used to watch the news every single day, but I got tired of hearing about Bin Laden and Sadam Hussein and all the other glorifying reports of killers and dictators. Maybe I perceive this wrong, but it seems like the major networks are more inclined to capture and broadcast evil doings of a killer or madman but when it comes to the goodness of people's deeds and the stories that had a wonderfully positive impact on other peoples' lives, it's no longer the crux of the highlight in the news. Whether people want to believe it or not, the vast majority of people in this nation and abroad are more likely to watch the news when the topics are about devastation, murder, fiascos or sexually explicit acts that have gained public attention and publicity. If there weren't any crimes occurring in the nation, it would have a world wind effect on the unemployment rate and when there's a high unemployment rate — it essentially affects the entire economy. As much as a lot of us would love to live in a society where we can co-exist amongst each other without violence and crime, evil is entirely too powerful. Even though some people may not be directly affected by violence and crimes, they're certainly not excluded from being directly affected.

The more crimes we have, the more prisons will be built, the more prisons, the more criminals will be incarcerated. Unfortunately, it's a cyclic evolution, and people should continue to contribute to the positive efforts that are being made to try to break and minimize some of these cycles occurring in communities and families. There are people who passionately fight for the cause of drug addiction prevention and safer streets, but of course, this is an on-going struggle that the activists are grappling with. People shouldn't be deterred or detracted from trying to save and help people dispel the yokes and strongholds that are destroying their lives; however, the task can be discouraging when you don't feel like you're seeing positive results especially in a certain time frame. A lot of people struggle with the regrettable notion that they are not doing enough to reach out or they could have done something differently to help even more. The devil will use guilt to plague our conscience and psyche which in turn you'll become a passive enabler that will create a counterproductive window to allow the person you're helping to drag you along with their problems.

People will use you as an emotional punching bag and exploit your compassion to precipitate and aid their endeavors and self-destruction; however, it's admirable how people dedicate their lives to help other people, but sometimes we have to let go of people who are emotionally draining us especially if they're not trying to help themselves. Sometimes we think we're helping people by trying to constructively micro-manage a person decisions or chasing behind them to get them to do right but in all actuality, in the certain instance, we're not helping at all by trying to diffuse, dispel or solve their problems People must endure certain things before they realize that a hard head makes a soft ass or a hot stove will burn their damn hands if they touch it. There's a universal language that sets the tone of how people interact and engage one another – there's a quid pro quo scenario of a symbiosis amongst each other, which is rare, or it's the typical use, abuse, and selfishly take, take, take and never really give. We as humans have to be careful and cautious in the manner of who we embrace because being indiscreet can be the detriment of our physical or emotional demise. Trust is essential, but it requires "time" to authenticate if "trust" is the language that could be potentially placed in the equation.

In prison, one person can do something that could affect the security of the operation, in which every prisoner could be placed on complete lock-down. One prisoner could be responsible for a certain privilege being taken away from everyone and of course, it doesn't seem fair, but that's how things operate in prison. Prime example, if a prisoner is stabbed on the other side of the compound, the entire prison could be placed on a lock down, and within a two week period every prisoner on the compound could be shaken down and stripped searched for shanks/knives. A shakedown consists of the guards disorganizing all your possessions by rummaging through your property like it has no value. Every time a warden allows us to do something like a privilege – someone always messes it up for everyone else, that's exactly why I don't care about any so-called 'prison privileges.' It's not a privilege to me if it's not involving educating yourself or learning to develop a closer relationship with God. Pacification with these prison privileges and amenities has nothing to do with helping prisoners with their problems from rehabilitative perspective. Prison officials are simply using incentives and disincentives to keep prisoners in compliance, with no real intent to try to reform or rehabilitate anyone. Most prisoners would be more content with more privileges because it would allow them to preoccupy their time without the boredom of being a factor in shifting their mental balance. Most prisoners prefer not to read, study or research because it's tedious to them and the tedium drives them up the wall. Boredom leads to thinking as crazy as this may sound, some prisoners don't even like to think to exercise their brain cells especially productively.

As much as prisoners complain about certain aspects of their imprisonment – The American Prison System is by far better than most prisons in the world. At least you're allowed to have rights in the American prison system despite most of the time your rights are violated. The mistreatment and impropriety that occurs conflicts with your rights, but it's not even a comparison of how prisoners are woefully treated in other countries in the world. Many nations don't care about a prisoner's rights, and in most prisons in the world, you don't have any rights. Prisons are modern day slave camps in most countries, and they travail prisoners like a slave in bondage.

In some countries, there's no refusal in working and death is almost certain to be the penalty for refusing to work – whether it be an execution or gradual starvation, death is inevitably imposed when you refuse to work in certain prisons in the world. A lot of prisoners think they're being oppressed in the American Prison System, in which they may be by the American Standards; However, prisoners are egregiously treated like animals and even tortured in other countries when they don't abide by the rules and prison regulations. I know this may sound crazy to a prisoner with paradoxical contents, but it's somewhat of a blessing to be in the American Prison system when you weigh the scale of the emotional and physical hardships you would endure in a prison system in another country with brutal tactics of a low tolerance for any defiance or resistance. Whether it's a prisoner, a criminal or a law-abiding citizen, most of the time we all will omit the fact, or fail to realize how blessed we are with the things we take for granted until we are placed in the situation where we can feel, see and understand what's like to live in a nation where it's difficult to have clean water to drink nevertheless food to eat – unless we're spiritual Christians, we would never understand the depth of our blessings.

Being in prison takes a psychological toll on your family as well because the physical and emotional separations can be emotionally draining. It's equally difficult when your significant other wants to be a part of your life but they simply can't within the tangibility parameters and realms, in which the prison gates poses constraints within their arms reach obviously. Mothers, grandmothers, aunts and your children usually are more affected by your incarceration than anyone else in your family because they're more prone to have an emotional connection with you. It's hard to watch your child grow up in prison because parents feel like there's so much their child could be doing with their lives instead of wasting their years away in prison. A parent can go through more stress than their child who's incarcerated and moreover, mothers tend to blame themselves for their child's criminal acts. Parents go through phases of regrets and self-pity, and this process could essentially stultify them in an emotional, financial or spiritual way. Usually, a parent may question themselves whether or not they were a good parent or if they could have done more to prevent their child from leading down the path of destruction. Either way, it's an emotional roller-coaster for anyone who cares for you and especially to those who wholeheartedly love you.

You can never get comfortable in prison because at any given second the administration can tell you to pack your things and you can be moved to another cell or unit on the compound of the prison or possibly get transferred to another prison. Usually, when you get transferred, you're either sent to a lower custody prison with more privileges, you can be sent to a higher security level prison with fewer privileges, or in some cases, you could be lateral to another prison with the same security level.

It's not psychologically or emotionally conducive to get attached to anyone because prison has a strange way of interfering with your psyche and the mental balance you create by embracing a fellow comrade. Having someone to do your time with within the confinements of prison could be paramount, but you still must remain objective and not subjective. Prison can be a very dreary and lonely purgatory in which good camaraderie can keep you afloat socially from going completely haywire. Of course, it's different folks for different strokes but if you're not a gang member, a Muslim, an addict, a reprobate/degenerate, or some sort of a perverted deviant — you're not going to get along with the vast majority of the prison population; moreover, there's not enough space to filter out the trash and poison you're surrounded by. Fortunately, I'm not a part of any of these categories and that in itself minimized my options for camaraderie. The truth of the matter I've always been a loner and I would rather subject myself to monotony than to have a fake engineered social circle. Becoming attached is not a favorable trait to have in prison, but I guess when you share similar common denominators of interest in your early beginning stages of imprisonment — it's understandable but still ill-advised.

Prison can make you psychologically and emotionally dependent on your family and even your comrade. It's a constant occurrence to get attached to people especially while establishing a dialogic rapport with that particular person. You can easily become despondently detached once you're separated from the person you've embraced. I'm certainly not remotely referring to any homosexuality bonds because you have some "thoroughbred" brothers who struggle with the same reality of the separation of their eternal friends within these prison walls. This environment is too dysfunctional for any stability whereas you become comfortable with your surroundings or your associate. Maybe it's confidence, but it seems like when you become relaxed or comfortable being in a certain housing unit, the prison administration could move you for some odd reasons and that's exactly why I'm always prepared to be moved at any given second.

Gang rivalries or gang related issues cause a lot of friction and tension in prison obviously and a lot of prisoners who aren't gang members, they feel a little uneasy. From my point of view and stance, all this mess is an animation to me because you have a bunch of followers following more followers. You have prisoners proclaiming to be a part of the infamous gangs like "Crips" or the "Bloods," and a lot of these gangs viably exist in their neighborhoods but when they come to a prison cell, all of a sudden they're self-proclaimed Crip or Blood. It's pathetic how desperate prisoners are becoming to be a part of something without a real cause of a movement. Usually, a youngster join a gang because they're fearful and they feel safe to be a part of a group that supposedly stick together, in which they can depend on one another. Most gang members, especially in the Virginia system, are lost in their ambivalence and misery and normally by the time they figure out how foolish they've been wasting their years away — the world is quite different. It doesn't make a difference what's a persons' status, affiliating membership or any conditions of their existence, if a person doesn't figure out the truth before they depart from this earth — the darkness of their abyss will never end.

After the September 11th attack, people were utterly appalled and disgusted with terrorists and criminals of abroad because this callous and calculating attack sent a radioactive shock wave across the nation and even the world. During that period the "leniency" for criminals made a paradigm shift in which it was more stiff harsher sentencing. Circuit court judges became outrageous with the number of years they were imposing on offenders and the stigmatic view on offenders and prisoners egregiously exacerbated. The Commonwealth of Virginia has some of the harsh Judges in the nation, and your race plays a role in the determining factor of the equality, justice, and fairness of the judicial system. A first time offender especially an African American who commits a violent crime can easily get twenty years or better and God knows the victim better not die because that's almost a guaranteed life-sentence or at least a considerable amount of years that's almost equivalent to a life sentence. A life sentence in Virginia is your natural life because there's no parole and without parole, you'll spend the remainder of your life in prison. Every prison has to do 85% to 91% of that original sentence, and that doesn't quantify or compute to 85%. One would have to speculate – if Judges are more inclined to give a criminal more time because they're aware by parole being abolished, more prisons would need to be built and more money to be made. Is this an overall political strategy to create revenues to boost the economy in the small towns where these prisons are located or are just a theory for which one factor has absolutely nothing to do with the other. Either way, it doesn't matter because ultimately the political figures will do whatever is necessary to keep these prisons filled as long as it doesn't flagrantly violate anyone's rights publicly.

Prison has opened my eyes to the thing I was once blind to see, and I've been able to examine myself and re-examine myself to the point that I've identified all my strengths and all my weakness. I was lost, and my outlook on life was surreal and abstract from the realization of my life. Naturally, I went through the maturation phase of changing, transforming and renewing myself and I don't think I would have been able to surpass the sophomoric barriers that distorted my perception. Prison undoubtedly was a serious life-defining wake-up call for me, and it's unfortunate how some of us dispel the obfuscation of our true essence and identity when it seems like it's nearly too late to be able to get another chance to live freely amongst those we love while allowing your positive energy to help others. My heart yearns for freedom, but considering the horrible things criminals and terrorists have done to people, there shouldn't be any exceptions for me either. I should suffer equally in my own, misery and purgatory because regardless how young I was I didn't appreciate life enough to respect the civil codes of living to love myself and my family; moreover, I didn't appreciate my freedom enough because I had broken the laws of the land.

I think the only people who are worthy of empathy or sympathy are those who haven't done anything wrong to be treated unfairly. Some people have suffered a long duration of imprisonment, and they were innocent. No one can understand your pain until they endure the similar heart-rending painful experiences you've endured and this pertains to everything in life. Every day someone is dying and suffering and as much as Americans complain about hardships, relationship trials, and errors – we're losing our awareness of the magnitude of our blessing on this American soil. Criminals complain in prison, and people in the society complain about frivolous things to each other to the point their actions would suggest that they're oblivious to how blessed they are, considering all sorts of debilitating world woefully afflict so many other countries, where chaos and mayhem is the crux of peoples enchanted lives.

A prison is a place for the spiritually dead people and the energy of the entities you're surrounded by can swarm you whereas you become a walking zombie. If you're striving to excel and you're trying to defeat your demons – prison makes it more difficult and in some instances almost unpracticed. Every day it's a test of your patience, your forbearance, and your restraint because you're surrounded by a bunch of people who exude negative energy all the time as if they harness it with a passion. Imagine how difficult it will be to take strides forward of your self-rehabilitation, but you're constantly being tempted to embrace your old ways with contagious instigators and deplorable. Imagine spending years walking around with venom in your veins when with your evil ways but now you've washed and extracted those impurities out of your body for which you're striving for spiritual elevation and cultivation to avoid so many evil distractions and entities in one location because the environment is congested with filthy predatory mentalities.

If you were brought up to be tough, violent and aggressive, it's easy to exhibit those traits because it's ingrained in your mind as part of your character. That is exactly how I was brought up, and the type of negative exposure I had with the violence and the killings in the ghettos only exacerbated the negative energy I've learned to harness in my heart like a carcinogenic. When your mind has been modeled with all sorts of negative traits and characteristics, it becomes like an affinity to be negative but when you've explored your mind, and you realized your heart longs for change within yourself, this is when you'll be tempted and tested from every angle of your mind when you're going through the process of deprogramming and deconditioning yourself. When you recondition yourself, it's imperative that you exercise the good virtues that you've never exercised before, but the problem is – you only can receive the formula and recipe to the virtues through God as his obedient child. Prisoners in prison will allow you to reflect on how negatively stupid and foolish you were and also it can be a reflection how determined you can be if you want to change and cleanse your heart and mind. Once you're able to grow, you can see through other people how you were in retrospect, in addition to that – you'll see how you were harboring so much ill-will negative garbage filtered in your heart. It's easy to get upset or frustrated when things don't go your way, but you possess power over your composure and your temper when you can honestly be unaffected by something that would normally make you perturbed and uneasy with yourself. It takes a considerable amount of willpower, patience, and humility to deal with an energy source that affects your pride, reputation, and ego punctuated by the masculinity testosterone especially when you're a target of provocation or instigating incitement.

The prison life will have you questioning yourself if you have a conscience to change. You'll get more in tune with understanding all your emotions but how you deal with it — is something each person will have to learn on their own while beseeching God's guidance. Most prisoners deal with their emotions by acting out aggressively or counterproductively with this contumacious attitude towards the guards, or whoever tries to regulate, micromanage or dictate their decisions. Most prisoners have psychological problems that are acute, and they really can't control their temper tantrums, inner rage or their inflammatory impulses of aggression. Most counselors and mental health employees aren't qualified to help prisoners effectively besides recommending medication; the employees cannot know how to engage with a person with problems oppose to approaching the person as a dehumanizing prisoner with objectified views. The sad part of it all, a lot of those youngsters would re-enter back into the society with a positive head on their shoulders, if they had qualified compassionate employees who know how to help people to change efficaciously. If a person doesn't want to change, obviously no effort or approach would be effective; however, it's political politics with a silhouette line of what's construed as fraternization and that in itself acts as a deterrence for counselors to breach any parameters that could suggest that they care about helping prisoners. Of course, a G.E.D. won't carry anyone very far in life especially being a convicted felon. However, it's a starting point wherefore it's the cornerstone of the beginning of their foundation. Unfortunately, without therapeutic treatments or rehabilitative, educational methods, it's almost hopeless for the youth in prison who has the opportunity to re-enter back into the society. The reality is, they're still struggling with the same problems prior to them coming to prison for which that essentially plated the role of leading them to prison and as a result, they're returning into the society with the same mindset. Only God will be able to save those who are completely lost, in which it's inevitable that they will become a part of a statistical recidivism rate because without God's help, death or return to prison is a promise.

Every day I wake up to this prison cell, and I ask myself "what is my purpose in life?" I wrestle with my reality for almost two decades in prison until it happened. I struggle with the fact that God may want me to spend a significant portion of my life in here to help others, but this was when I was groping in my darkness looking for answers. I'm strong, but I didn't feel like I was strong enough to grow old in prison and watch my family have a life without me being a part of it. I realized life is not about what we want; it's not about our selfish fulfilments or glorification. Therefore if we think like that, then we're indubitably lost. Life is not about us, it's about the servitude of our God, and it's a phenomenal sacrifice to be a servant of God opposed to living a life enjoying all the thrills of gratifying the flesh. I now know and understand the righteous cause of our creation, and I know it's difficult for God. I'm not a devoutly religious person; however I am a strong believer of Jesus Christ sacrifice and immolation, and this (time) in prison has been an awakening revelatory experience. Living to please the flesh is quite easy but living to serve God is more arduously challenging than anything known to man especially without serious faith, condemnation will inevitably fail us, but consecration will inevitably resurrect us to fulfill our purpose to serve God.

There are a lot of people who are trapped in their emotional capsule of prisons. People are physically free, but emotionally or spiritually they're captive to their mental cage, and one of the worst aspects of being in prison is suffocating mentally, while coping with the physical imprisonment. There have been millionaires who've committed suicide because they were bleeding inside with incompleteness of a void in their hearts in which most people believe (money) is the ultimate problem-solving the solution for everything.

Usually, a psychologist will try to give their analytical, diagnostic point of view of why an affluent person or celebrity would foolishly commit suicide but the truth of the matter; you'll never know how a person is feeling about their life until they reveal it to you. Prison isn't the ideal environment to go around speaking about your problems obviously and just like the average law-abiding citizens, people, in general, would like to have someone they can trust to express and confide in. Generally, people struggle and are unable to find solutions to help themselves with their problems, and unfortunately, that's exactly why so many young people are coming to prison, committing suicide and even getting murdered in the streets. Believe it or not, a lot of people's problems could be either solved, dealt with effectively or disentangled with just a little encouragement, guidance and motivation. Of course, some people may require more than just a little support, but the point is — some lives could be saved by a simplified approach as opposed to a convoluted approach. It may be difficult to be receptive to my insight because I am in fact incarcerated and the stigmatic cloud is over my head, but my book of life on this planet is not over yet.

There's always bed space available for criminals even if they have to make bed space but prison shouldn't always be the solution. Unfortunately, most people think prison is the best viable solution for any perpetrator until their child does something wrong that may require them to go to prison. Every youthful offender can't be saved obviously, but there could be a better alternative or therapeutic solutions for young offenders who can potentially be reformed. Some states have been in debt because they've spent too much money on building prisons. In all actuality they'll probably never stop building prisons and considering Virginia and Florida has abolished parole, it's likely that prisons will be the economic shift detrimentally or productively, wherefore there's going to be more jails and prisons than hospitals, treatments centers and universities combined. Prisons are the new forts, and the irony of this is based on the required security measures architecturally and infrastructure-wise, prisoners will be more likely to survive the first wave of a cataclysmic disaster oppose to the average law-abiding citizens home. Prisons are not acting as a catalyst for change, and it's certainly not acting as deterrence or decreasing the criminal statistic rates. Prisons are simply warehouses in which for economic and political purposes, men and women are being housed there indefinitely, permanently or conditionally; however, it's not helping the society by carrying millions of men and women behind bars when there are other alternative methods to help men and women become productive citizens. The sociologic construct of the mindset of politicians is utterly abstract because they feed the public this smokescreen of an objectified pursuit to de-escalate and decrease criminal activities, but then they conceal their true agendas of being investing partners with the very people who are privatizing prisons as a corporation.

Each day I try to remind myself that things could be a lot worse. I have my physical health and mentally intact and more importantly I have spiritual soundness. It was cool to be a knucklehead and rebel against anyone who got in the way of me being the oppositional devil that I was. I was young, foolish, naïve, and fortunately, I've grown up spiritually, and I understand the seriousness of what we can offer to life. If you want to defeat your demons in here or out there, you must have on a protective shield and armor by God to help you rebuke those persistent demons because the negativity and wickedness circulate in the air like a biological toxic chemical weapon. Prison is one of the devil's resting spot and it's easy for the devil to plant seeds of evil. In prison or anywhere in the world, you are required by God to continuously meditate, pray and read the word because the devil stays on the rise to ruin and destroy everything he can get his hands on. It took nearly 18 years to really grasp the concept of prayer because prior to me giving my life to God — my pursuit was mundanely motivated in which ultimately it was in vain.

There have been times I've been on the verge of killing another prisoner for an infringement that didn't quite constitute murder, but for the sake of my growth and family, I've managed to control my homicidal impulses and negative ideation. Fortunately, I haven't been disrespected by anyone because my temper has always been my downfall, I would react so swiftly, and violently that by the time a person realize what's occurring, it would be too late. Even in prison, I've inflicted injuries upon people and the only reason I had impunity because my attacks upon a person would be strategically planned out as an attempt to circumvent the video footage or eyewitness account; however, sometimes I wasn't strategic, I just reacted in the manner of what was required. It's a blessing how I've been able to make improvements with transformation strides. My heart was fed up with being evil and always quick to respond in an aggressive, violent manner, which in turn would be counterproductive to any aspirations or goals I had. I was raised and brought up with the type of caliber of individuals in prison, so it was natural like an affinity for me to fit in with the mindset of being a leader in prison. In retrospect, I was lost, but I tried to intellectualize things, by trying to give some sort of explanation for my actions justifiably.

Holidays in prisons remind me how precious your freedom is. I don't care about any human-made material things because being with your family is priceless and nothing can substitute for that. Life is too short to be wasting and squandering years in prison. You can't replace those youthful years of your life, and you certainly can't replace that time you missed being apart from your families' life. Most people believe that if you take a life, you don't deserve to have a life or a second chance but who should be able to determine that. Life and living are precious and irreplaceable, therefore when you take away the profundity of allowing a person to live, essentially you're disrupting the cycle of creation and living, by murdering people. The consensus is, if you rob someone out of the time they could have with their families that they could have savored and enjoyed, why should you be able to. I think a murderer be judged by the factual basis and circumstances that subsequently led to how and why the murder was committed. I think the immediate family members of the victim should ultimately determine if the perpetrator will ever be worthy of forgiveness or leniency, and I don't think anyone else's opinion should be valued or considered; however, as equally as you want God to forgive you, you have to forgive, but forgiving doesn't constitute a lenient sentence to be imposed. Those are determining factors should be appropriately rendered and adjudicated by the decree of the courts.

It's extremely difficult to accept the actuality or even the eventuality of life and to live in prison indefinitely or permanently because you have no sense of fulfillment of knowing that your purpose in life is worthy of your existence. Every day there's a vibe of sullenness, every day there's a vibe of uncertainty in the longevity of their lives, every day there's a vibe of harnessed tension and misplaced frictional energy and static. It's a lot easier to the front with this façade as if you're unaffected by your circumstances but that will only last for so long. The only prisoners who will be truly affected by their incarceration are the ones who have a conscience to change because they love their families and they learned to love God and themselves. Any prisoner who accepts prison as their reality till death and they don't have God in their heart. They're simply a product of an institutionalized mindset, and their physical existence is like vapor in the air doomed to the brimstone. This is not my reality, and I refuse to accept growing old in prison mentally or physically. My fate is in my hands, but my expiation and piacular is required to restore and renew myself on faith to God. I'm going to serve and oblige God's purpose for me because I choose not to have this numbness in my spine with the uncertainty of what's in store for my life. My physical freedom is not my salvation. My spiritual and mental freedom is my deliverance in which I'm thirsty for wholeheartedly.

In my belief system, I have two options, I can trust God to guide and deliver me to my salvation while I serve God accordingly or I can selfishly fribble my time with the mundane things on this planet and end my physical misery to the eventuality of my physical demise. I feverishly want my life to feel purposeful, and I want to be able to help make a difference in someone's life, but I would be lying if I was remised to declare sympathy, leniency or clemency – people of goodwill meet those criteria. Even though my heart has changed and my outlook on life has resoundingly changed the lens of my psyche, my circumstances will remain the same until God almighty feel like I'm required to endure tests, trials, and tribulations as the newly transformed sheep to God. Our choices are what is expected in life and most of the times that coincide with our fate. Accountability is the way of life, and whether it's individually or systematically, if you can't handle the consequences for your actions, you shouldn't do the wrong things. I've come to terms with the responsibility of my action and I used to think it was unfortunate that I was unable to astray from the path that ultimately led me to prison, however, the immutable fact is; prison saved my life, and it was already written by God to save me out a particular juncture and season.

Prison can make your brain rot in a rut if you inhale the debilitating poison that's corroding through the minds of the atmosphere. Prison can make you lose your hope and your desire to live, and keeping your sanity intact can be painstakingly challenging at times. People have to learn to internalize God's love and your families' love while fighting inner and outer demons trying to feed off you like a maggot to destabilize your grounded balance. It's convoluted to appreciate life when you don't feel like you're having and it's hard to love yourself when you don't feel worthy of being loved. Prison can take you through emotional shambles to the point it's overwhelming to breathe in the very oxygen that sustains your body. It's ineffable to feel the buoyancy of life because you don't know how it feels to be alive anymore especially when you walk around with a dead heartbeat, with your bones scattered on the yard. Invariably, God has already set the tone, but the question one would have to ask oneself is; do you know the angelic words to the heavenly euphoric songs or have you acclimatized yourself to the dysphoria that sets by Satan's plan. It's senseless to try to justifiably misattribute God's deity because his love is never questionable or inauthentic. The people you entrust dearly as your asserted confidant will be the ones you should question the authenticity of their love. We can try to moralize people or even unjustifiably sexualize people justifiably but one thing we can't do, we can't actualize an illusion to insult God or diminish the sacrifice of Jesus Christ.

Is crime changing our society? Probably so. Or has the society forgotten that carnage and mayhem of war and crime have always existed? Or has violence migrated to certain corners of the planet that was once shielded communities that were protected in a capsule in which for decades, those who were protected never experienced or endure ordeals of being plagued by the bloodshed of criminals and miscreants? Is building prisons helping our society? Probably not because there's always another criminal to replace predecessor and successor, but when you think about the increase of violence and the government or the private owners benefitting off criminals violent offenses to go to prison, it's hard to say anything that wouldn't have grounds for an argument or debate. I'm certainly not trying to have a synopsis on the basis of a racial dichotomy or bifurcation but roughly in the last 50 years tens of thousands of black people were murdered in their own congested poverty-stricken neighborhoods; therefore from the sociologic standpoint, it appears that the politicians that convene in D.C. and abroad, has dispassionately ignored the staggering statistics rates for decades. After the inhuman devastation of the terrorist attack of Sept 11, 2001, it seemingly appears that every circuit Judge that oversees the regions of the underprivileged neighborhoods in the black communities; those judges were imposing harsher sentences on the blacks disproportionately oppose to the whites. Of course, this topic is arguably controversial due to the propaganda and disinformation that's been disseminated as a way to marginalize or overshadow the activists who diligently advocate for awareness and change.

Martin Luther King Jr. gave his, "I have a dream" speech in 1963 and when you think about those iconic activists who adamantly fought for our rights that cost them their lives, I feel like a pitiful example of a person who didn't have enough dignity for myself, for those who love me and for those countless of individuals who lost their lives and sacrificed so much. Blood in the sand has always been a token of expression of sacrifice, and many lives were sacrificed for black people to be accepted equally. It's an egregious disservice to our people for us young black individuals to be ungrateful for the dedication and commitment of the struggles of the movement that our ancestors and elders fought so passionately for. Words can't adequately delineate or express how awful I felt once I finally realized that my actions were utterly reproachable with a shameless smack to the face to those who fearlessly fought and died for my justice, equality and more importantly for my freedom. Even Jesus sacrificed his life by voluntarily allowing his blood to be shed for our sins and yet most of us will live on this planet bickering and complaining without never shedding one drop of blood for the sake of God.

I never thought I would be able to embrace the purities in my soul because my flesh practically buried everything beneath the contaminated garbage that was being filtered through my bloodstream from this ominous misguidance of the streets. In retrospect I hated who I've become in the eyes of others, I hated all the evil contaminations in my flesh, and nothing would be more fulfilling to me in life but to have my flesh cleansed from all the impurities and imperfections. I've learned to despise evil because it's gradually destroying everything. We're destroying the trees, the oceans, the air and everything in this entire planet. The tycoons, moguls and colossal billionaires are drilling, and digging holes of every corner of the planet and just for the sake of supplying the demand of consumers; people are willing to be rich now regardless if the planet being destroyed gradually. Most billionaires don't give a damn what may or may not happen in 100 years. Their only concern is making money at present to ensure they remain affluent with an outrageous opulence more than they need for several lifetimes.

My existence is oblivious, in which I'm a statistical mark, labeled with an identification number of the state prison system. That label alone is characterized as the lowest of the scum on the planet besides the terrorists. God has inserted something into my spirit on Nov 24, 2015, and it was like a renascent life-changing experience that was the epiphany to the perplexities of my mind. Whatever was symptomatic to my problems is now inconsequential to my deliverance because God gave me a favor even when I didn't deserve it. Before giving my life to God, I couldn't breathe in life because I gave up my choices at a young age, so I was breathing in death. Breathing in death was ascribed to my unwillingness to change and as each day passed by I question whether or not I was worthy enough to have the privilege of breathing. To most people, being alive is a privilege and a blessing, but to others, it can be a curse. I didn't love life enough to grow old in prison while watching my loved ones die as the years go by. I was indifferent about living anyway, and I questioned God on some occasions, simply inquiring about why he didn't let me die in the streets. Of course, I wrestled with this notion for nearly two decades before I had my moment with God. Before my covenantal declaration to God, I had homicidal and suicidal ideations quite often. I felt like no matter how educated or knowledgeable you may be or become while being in prison, your existence was only meaningful to those who love you, and your contribution to life is within the realms of the prison gates. To look back in hindsight, admittedly it would be irreverent to be remised to thank God especially if you had a fair share of pain, close calls to death or an unbelievable transformation from being an unconscionable deplorable person to being a renewed child of God.

Prison is prison whether it's physical or mental and living and dying without fulfilling your purpose is a waste of human existence. When you're in an environment with people who have their standards, normative and their own criminal ethics for which it sounds like a paradox but the normalcy of what people learn to accept in prison is unrighteously outrageous, and I refuse to allow my perception on life to be tainted and further with this nonsense. I would rather be on a deserted island with books, pens, and paper than to be amongst this sort of filth. I was once a part of this filth that travels and pervades through us humans, but this perpetuity of this cycle must stop somewhere. My flesh yearns for physical freedom, but I would rather depart from this earth from a deserted island serving my Lord and savior than to be physically free as a perpetrator of the streets with hypocrisy. Life can be a mysterious puzzle that you will have to figure out for yourself, and if you choose not to invite God into your life, your puzzle will remain a mystery, and it will never be solved.

Prison is a physical purgatory and if you want to enjoy life with the bliss of God's blessing don't play in the devil's nest or the snake's pit. I played in the devil's nest, and now my punishment is worthy of my piacular. Sometimes there's only one chance we'll have in life, and if you're indiscreet, you'll miss out on your chance. It is better to embrace love because anything else is death. The world is a place that we live and co-exist at, and regardless of how many fortresses we build, nothing can stop the devil's wrath but God, and time is of the essence. A prison is a place that confines criminals who live a certain lifestyle but evil can never be confined, and I certainly can't be a part of it any longer. Initially, these shackles shattered me, but I subscribed to my resurgences in which my pain is no longer in the rain. The psychodynamics of my unwavering pursuit to serve God will enable me to destigmatize and dispel the stigma that sometimes stifles people's progress in the world. We have to be convalescent, resilient and perseverant through our faith in God because war is beyond the relativism of what the preconceive ideologies and assumptions are for which is generally intellectualize or rationalize their actions.

God can mystify you and spark a phenomenal surge in you to catapult you to an oasis that will make you feel unbelievably peaceful, joyful and remarkably blissful! I am divinely favored, God has truly given me something that I haven't yet maximized my horizon of spiritual exploration. I humbly and honorably accept the responsibility as a righteous solder for God. I'm learning the process of loving for which I've been an emotional virgin my entire life because I know nothing about love and I thought God only required faith and righteousness until I read I Corinthians 13:2. This particular scripture introduced me to something that I had no experience in because my cavalier attitude was equivalent to an extra hybrid. God is exceptionally extraordinary and incomprehensibly loving to his children.

May the journey begin to serve and love.

Author

Mr. Carlton Clay

I was sixteen years old when I was first introduced to the confinement of an adult jail cell. I was illiterate, uneducated, uncontrollable, and utterly unstable. Throughout the years of the imprisonment, I learned to self-educate myself because I felt this inexplicable energy within me to change. I'm a part of this microwave generation, but my heart isn't tainted with this breed of ignorance that's being embedded into the youth's minds. The irony of this experience, I would have unquestionably been killed in the streets of the ghettos, and I would have never been able to reach the growth of my spiritual and intellectual elevation.

I was a product of the perpetuity of the common acceptance of ignorance. I abhorred the fact that I was statistically deemed to fail, but at the same token, I lacked the education and intelligence to be able to see through the obscurity of my misguidance. Typically, we try to point a finger at someone for our indiscretions and mistakes but realized that I'm the blame-worthy for my own choices regardless of my upbringing. Accepting the responsibility for our actions is the first step towards growth. Even though I had my fair share of mishaps, and I was egregiously abused emotionally and physically, I still had hope for deliverance. Like most youngsters in the ghettos, I was rebellious and oppositional towards anyone who attempts to try to control me.

My contumacy was a direct result of a child feeling unloved by the biological entities that brought me into this world. The dysfunctional environment and household only exacerbated the hate I harbored in my heart. There are no excuses to be made. What led me to this psychological and emotional persecution is irrelevant. Yesterday is gone, and we can't allow our negative past to dictate our positive choices and decisions in the future.

Without a question of a doubt, I'm paying the price for my transgressions, and despite what people categorically think about a convicted felon in prison, I am a person who breathes in life and, I'm a person who will be judged beyond the "Judgment of man."

Day after day mothers and fathers will lose their children unexpectedly from the violence of others, and it's so unfortunate and sad how many young black people are dying before they were able to know what life really offered and what they could offer to life. Most poverty-stricken environments are the devil's nest because the drugs and alcoholism permeate through the air that they breathe in. The inevitability of the contamination being spread and embedded into the youth's minds will unequivocally be unfathomable until people stop just talking about what needs to be done and just try to do it.

Of course, no one can save them all or even majority of them, but a lot of people don't realize the gift and power they have to offer the inspirational empowerment to a lost soul. Regardless of their tough façade of nonchalance and apathy, a lot of the youth in the black communities need to feel loved, but they hide their emotional side behind their aggression. A lot of the youngsters are too psychologically imbalanced to reach out to them if you're not qualified or capable of approaching them in a certain way whereas they don't become offensive and reject your help and support.

In most cases, prison is the only place where you can contain a certain amount of evil in a person, Regardless of their age, race, or gender, some people can't cope and function in a world that have laws and consequently, they must be confined to a prison for the rest of their natural life. As long as the devil exist, there will always be violence, murder, and havoc. We can only try to live our lives to survive even in the midst of the devil's wickedness and evil. Living in the dark shadows of evil, propels us to choose to be a part of it or rebuke it. Life is too short for emotional nonsense, stress, depression, and despair but unfortunately sometimes it comes with the territory just by co-existing with others we can waste our lives waiting for a miracle to fall in our laps, or we can strive in faith with the determination to excel in life.

There's nothing unique about me, I breathe just like the next human, and I'm alive because of my choices and decisions but mainly because "God" isn't ready for me yet and the devil hasn't been able to stop the blood from circulating in my heart. As much as I would love to feel like I'm worthy of having a voice that carries enough weight to help someone, I'm not too sure about the power that exists in me.

As long as we're alive, we can develop a relationship with God but that's a choice we will ultimately have to make. Throughout my imprisonment, I've realized how blessed I am, but I've also learned to really understand and know who I am. I hated the person I become, and I was tired of being hateful, evil, violent, aggressive, negative, depressed, bitter, and lost. Yesterday is gone and the next hour is not promised to any of us.

Living can feel like you're already in hell because each step we take can either get easier or harder and unfortunately, a lot of people will not even get the opportunity to take enough step forward to look back and say, "I've come this far."

Prison is just a human-made building with razor-wire gates around it, but when you're in prison inside your mind, living is like a curse each day you will feel emotionally paralyzed. Yesterday is gone, and you have a choice, don't jeopardize and risk your freedom for nothing, because being with your family is monumentally priceless.

Even if you don't have a family,

There's love waiting to find you......

www.ingramcontent.com/pod-product-compliance
Lightning Source LLC
Chambersburg PA
CBHW070026260726
48658CB00002B/510